Facets *of* Love

Facets of Love

Ritu Chowdhary

PARTRIDGE
A Penguin Random House Company

To order additional copies of this book, contact
Partridge India
000 800 10062 62
orders.india@partridgepublishing.com

www.partridgepublishing.com/india

CONTENTS

In loving memory of my mother...

May we so love
as never to have occasion to repent
of our love!

HENRY DAVID THOREAU

ACKNOWLEDGEMENT

I WOULD LIKE TO EXPRESS my gratitude to my revered uncle Mr J K Tiwari, father of one of my close friend Hina, who really inspired me to initiate writing. I'm highly indebted to my father for ensuring that this book sees the light of the day. He has been my motivation throughout the project and a source of unrelenting moral support.

I would like to gratefully acknowledge the enthusiastic support extended by my brother, Puneet, in editing this book and a dear friend Neerja for her valuable suggestions from time to time.

Last but not the least, my husband and my little angel, Anya, who supported and encouraged me in spite of all the time it took me away from them.

Finally, my thanks to everyone, who have been with me through the course of this book.

CHAPTER 1

*S*HE'S TOO NERVOUS. THIS is her first day at college. Every sort of thought is running through her mind.

She's Sara Sanial; sweet, gentle and soft hearted, but undeniably pugnacious if you tell her boys are in any way better than girls.

Everywhere in the college, seniors were hunting for freshers — you might be able to guess the reason!

Sara had attended the first lecture and was rushing back to the hostel; her eyes were tied to the ground, notebook compressed in her folded arms and clinging to her body, each step covering a mile. She was afraid of being ensnared by seniors.

All of a sudden, she observed a shadow coming from the opposite side. "Oh God, I'm caught and that too, a guy. I'm going to give him a piece of my mind. Ragging is not good, hitherto we freshers are under so much stress and to add on to it, this harassment!"

He just passed by her and for a second they saw each other. At the moment Sara didn't know it, but this glance was going to change her life forever.

She felt happy that she had reached the hostel without anyone realizing it. Sara was safe for the day. She rushed to her room and met her two roommates, Supriya and Nancy. Supriya and Nancy were both from Mumbai. From what she could see, they seemed quite decent and cool. The three girls acknowledged mutual admiration for each other with a smile.

But Sara was restless. She had for the first time ventured out of her home, so she thought that maybe it was the anxiety of leaving her comfort zone that made her feel this way. And to top it off, the fear of the ragging on campus was continually nagging her mind.

20th August 2005, 7:30 a.m.: Sara was at the hostel mess table gulping her breakfast. She was feeling sick due to stress. She just swallowed the food, not appreciating that her breakfast time used to be some of the best moments she shared with her Mamma.

When she reached her room, she became stumped about what clothes to wear. 'I should look simple and humble; I shouldn't catch anyone's attention.' She decided to wear a black jeans and a light blue cotton shirt. Sara didn't realize it, but she was looking more beautiful than ever—as they say 'beauty lies in simplicity'.

She made it to her classroom right on time, anxious to meet her classmates. Students started entering the class, a few were exchanging smiles, others just wanted to rush inside and occupy a seat. There were only two girls in the group. No wonder! It was a mechanical engineering class. Girls used to be a rare species in that jungle.

Last to enter was the guy with whom Sara had shared a glance the previous day. He had an expressionless, carefree face, and exuded an impression into the classroom, like, "Oh what a favor I have done to the class by coming here and that too, so early in the morning".

Everyone stood up as Professor Pratap Gupta entered the class. As any normal academic practitioner, he started, 'Good morning class, welcome to the college! This is beginning of a new life for all of you. Hard work done today can reward you tomorrow, so take these years very seriously and focus on your studies. Hopefully no one is harassing you on the campus.'

A loud voice echoed in the room, 'Yes babies, these years will never come back, so make it a point to enjoy your whole day in the college and have as much fun as you can in the class.'

The professor shouted, 'Who was that?' There was a pin drop silence.

'Okay Sidhant! Get out of my class at once. Yes, you have no choice but to enjoy your day here. You might have planned to be an indispensable member of this class.'

Sara looked back. He was the same guy, who got up and moved out of the room with rock-solid confidence, as if suggesting, "Follow my steps if you want to be successful". Sara felt mesmerized and surely wanted to follow him.

Professor Gupta was able to identify Sidhant's peculiar voice. He was in his interview panel, and he was not keen to approve of his application due to his erratic candidature. Sidhant had completed two years of studies in economics, and in his third year realized that he didn't really enjoy this balancing act of demand and supply. He wanted to do something more macho, so he switched over to mechanical engineering.

The professor gave an overview of the subject and the class's year end goals. It went well and everyone perceived it as start of a new life, 'college life!' You always look forward to college, as this is also the entry to other new and important facets of life; adulthood, career, marriage....

Everyone came out of the lecture room and many were whispering about Sidhant. They were discussing his past and his bold-faced confidence amazed them.

Sara exchanged greetings with her only girl classmate, Avni Singh. They decided to go to the canteen and chat over a cup of tea. A few of their other classmates joined them.

The canteen looked like a crumbled old monument, surrounded by trees and bearing testimony to incalculable moments of the past: the good and bad times, the start and end of countless love stories, college politics, stressful campus interviews, and the excitement of employment packages being offered. Sara and Avni sat there, a little hesitant, and ordered their tea.

It wasn't long, of course, before a bunch of senior goons came around and started their fun time of picking on the freshman students.

Sara was getting nervous, but tried to put up a brave face.

One fellow said, 'Oh ma'am! You in the blue shirt, introduce yourself, and then tell, amongst us whom would you like to marry?' Sara got furious but then saw someone watching her with his expressionless face — none other than Sidhant. She felt his presence and it made her confident. This helped her to handle those goons with alacrity.

'Marriage is not a topic for my consideration as I have decided never to marry—so there's no question of making any choice.' The seniors had nothing to say to this answer.

Sidhant got up from there and Sara watched him leave. For a moment she wondered why he left so suddenly, but then Avni and she began talking about other things over their tea.

As time went on, Sara and Avni both proved to be sincere students, very particular about their attendance at lectures. Sara used to be in tiff, now and then, with her batch mates on mass bunk.

The boys, as usual, were always in a mood to enjoy their life and above all, their "godfather" Sidhant displayed it best. Every boy in the class seemed to be appreciative of Sidhant and there was little, if any, jealousy toward him for his carefree attitude towards life.

First semester exams started, and Avni and Sara competed in a friendly way to top each other. Sara topped the class and Jimmy, as he was popularly known, was the second topper. Avni had a crush on Jimmy and was honestly chasing him hard. He was a geek, much like Sara and often misread as to have no interest in girls.

Sidhant flunked two subjects but he marveled at the fact that he'd cleared the remaining seven. It wasn't that he was unable to cope up with engineering, but he just decided to give himself some rest. He spent more time sleeping than in attending classes and preparing for exams.

Everyone congratulated Sara for her grades and asked for a treat. It was decided whole class of thirty would meet at the college's favorite restaurant 'Aroma'. The party would be hosted by the first three toppers as they would also be eligible for merit scholarship.

7:00 p.m.: It was a nice evening at Aroma. Everyone was having a gratifying time over drinks, and cracking lots of jokes. Suddenly Sara asked, 'Where's Sidhant? Why didn't he come?' There were a few exchanged glances and one fellow answered, 'He might be sleeping'. Sara smiled and then tried to appear disinterested; she realized she may have looked overeager about Sidhant's whereabouts.

That night was undoubtedly bad for Sidhant in the boy's hostel. He was the talking point for everyone there, as the boys mimicked Sara showering all her love on Sidhant. The whole scene was quite awkward for him. He had never imagined anything like that in the faintest of his thoughts. But with bunch of hooligans around you, it's better to be quiet. Unfortunately, they mistook Sidhant's silence on the subject to be reinforcement of their taunts. Apparently he couldn't win either way.

Innocent Sara had no intentions of giving special attention to Sidhant. But as he was invariably odd man out, so Sara unintentionally, and out of curiosity asked about him without realizing what it could mean for her future.

The rest of that week Sidhant tried to avoid Sara, but there was something in her which made him ill-at-ease. For her part, she generally loathed guys like him, who were always clumsily dressed, chain smokers, non-serious about studies and in fact flawed in every which way. Never mind that he disrespected his professors and continuously acted snobbish.

One day Sara was sitting with Avni and Jimmy in the canteen. She realized Sidhant was also sitting in the corner staring at her as if he had frozen. Sara took her eyes off him and tried to chat with her friends. She was upset with this gesture of Sidhant's, which she perceived as disgraceful and undignified.

The very next day was Saturday and surprisingly Sidhant approached Sara and asked for her Thermodynamics notes. As Sara was already annoyed with him since yesterday, she refused to give the notes to him saying she would need to read them on the weekend. As an afterthought, Sara politely told Sidhant that he could have them on Monday if he was genuinely interested in reading them. Sidhant gave her a blank look and went away.

That weekend Sara came home. She was perturbed the whole weekend at her reaction, and didn't even touch her Thermodynamics notebook.

On seeing her disquiet, Sara's mother asked if everything was okay at college, to which she replied, 'A little tired Mamma.' Mom could see that it was something more than tiredness; she was mentally upset. As mother's will, she tried to dig a little deeper into it with Sara but the girl just put off her mother's efforts.

Monday morning after reaching college, the first thing Sara did was look for Sidhant. He wasn't there; maybe he was sleeping somewhere like usual, she thought. He came around in the afternoon and Sara rushed towards him as if she had come there only to meet him.

'Sidhant, you wanted these jottings', Sara said. He, without saying anything just looked at her and took the diary from her hand. Sara found him rude but she ignored it with an embarrassing smile. She realized that she was getting too sensitive about him.

It was a chilly day and the whole class was sitting outside on the college porch, basking in the sun. Sara sat with Avni discussing about next lecture's tutorials. A few guys were standing on their heads, striving to find out what were they talking about; others were laughing amidst themselves; the rest acted over smart to catch Sara and Avni's attentions. Sidhant sat just across them under the tree following his one point program of staring at Sara. Sara saw him and turned red with anger. She perceived he was doing it intentionally, to create a scene and make her an agenda of discussion amongst the boys. She got up from there and went to the lecture room for the next class to start. Again he irked her, and she got suspicious that he would use her notes to fabricate some story among the boys.

After the class, Sara went back to the hostel, upset and grumbling, "What does he think of himself? Idiot, it's only because of his attitude he is here, capricious". Tears started flowing out of her eyes. She realized she was on the road and people were watching her. She was astonished at her behavior.

Sara thought of teaching him a lesson. She heard someone calling her from behind. 'Sara, Sara'. She looked back to find Avni approaching her. Avni angrily said, 'Why didn't you wait for me? I looked for you all over the campus. God bless Sidhant, he told me that he saw you going towards the hostel".

Sara kicked her foot but kept on walking quietly. She straight away went to her room and threw herself on her bed. She brooded about the day's happenings and discerned that she was overreacting.

Later, Sara had a cup of tea, called Avni and went back to the college for their workshop.

Workshops were a perpetual source of fun time for the guys, and a stressful activity for Sara and Avni — especially Sara. They were making a chisel that day. The class attendant unceasingly helped the girls. He took small pieces of iron rod, heated them in the furnace for them. Their classmates were telling him, 'Rawat ji, let them do it on their own or else how would they learn?'

Sara always got offended with such remarks and promptly said, 'Rawat ji, they are right, we can do it on our own.' God of strength appeared in her during such situations and every time, surprisingly, she came out as a winner. Probably, Sidhant was correct when he called Sara an egoistic girl; but at times her ego was her source of willpower.

Rawat ji, told both of them, "Madam ji, pick up these hammers and strike it on the edges of these rods. Use as much force as you can to make good quality chisels. Guys surrounded them in a circle to see what would happen. These were not ordinary hammers, they were huge and heavy. It was difficult to even raise them.

Sara tried picking it up but couldn't even move it. A few chaps were smirking. One or two chauvinists came forward and said, 'Sara, we will also help you.'

'No, thank you'.

Next time, she picked up the hammer as if it was feather light and smashed it with great force on the rod.

'Good stroke', a guy said.

And the result was an 'A' grade chisel. On the contrary, Avni was content to work with Jimmy to complete the task.

Sidhant wasn't in the workshop. Sara realized she felt more composed with him not there.

Avni remarked, 'What a hectic day. I'm so tired, let's go to the canteen and relax for some time.'

Jimmy was gung ho on the idea of spending few moments with these two young ladies. They went to the canteen and the girls made themselves comfortable on the bench under the tree while Jimmy ordered, 'Mohan bahiya 3 cups'.

Like a magician, Sidhant appeared from somewhere and handed over the Thermodynamic notes to Sara. He was absolutely inanimate. He didn't utter a single word, not even 'thank you', and went away. Sara found this behavior too rude but didn't comment in front of Avni and Jimmy.

Around 6 o'clock they went back to their respective hostels.

Sara and Avni reached the hostel and some of their friends were sitting in a circle gossiping about everything going on around the college. They were discussing boys, professors and the relationship stages of all the couples. Avni found it interesting, and insisted Sara joins them in their girl's talk. Sara found it all grotesque as she was never the one to gossip about other people.

Sara was finding everything boring, and then a girl asked Avni about Sidhant. 'How is he? He should have been my classmate.'

Neha immediately said, 'Perhaps mine too had the sense prevailed on him a year back.'

There were giggles all around. Sara was hurt but couldn't understand why. The other day, she herself had labeled him a vacillating person, and now when everyone was referring to the same thing, she didn't appreciate it.

Neha said, 'He's a big loafer; he doesn't respect women and is interested in only one matter — s-e-x.'

This ongoing gossip made Sara uncomfortable, and she left for her room. While thinking about the discussion, she started flipping through her Thermodynamics notes and to her shock she found written on one of the pages:

> "We are all born sexual creatures, thank God, but it's a pity so many people despise and crush this natural gift."

Sara jumped out of her bed and shouted aloud, 'How dare him? Everyone is so right about him, he's a typical loafer!' Sara decided not to discuss it with anyone.

The next morning was fine. The weather was pleasant, a little cold, which anyone would have loved in those lush green surroundings. When Sara got up in the morning, her mood was calm and enthusiastic for the day ahead. She wanted to dress up nicely. She decided to wear a simple peach colored cotton salwar kameez and for a change, pearl studs.

When she looked in the mirror she wanted to tell herself, 'You are looking gorgeous dear.'

Everyone at the breakfast table appreciated her looks, and asked her what the special occasion was.

When Avni saw her, she gasped and said, 'So finally ma'am, you are out of that shell of yours and ready to make a killer entry into college life. I don't know how many guys are going to have a crush on you today.'

Sara smiled, appreciating the compliments.

As they entered the college, every face, including the professors, turned towards Sara. It seemed, at least for once, they all wanted to appreciate her. They were wondering if everything was ok with her. Her biggest educational admirer, Dr Pratap Singh seemed disappointed to see her join in the queue of modern world Juliet's who come to college only to find their Romeos.

Both of them, Avni and Sara entered the class. It became difficult for her to handle the surprised and obvious stares that spread all across the room. Interestingly, Sidhant was also there early in the class that day, however he totally ignored her.

Sara took her seat and turned her face towards the white board. Something was scribbled there which she started reading.

"No matter how plain a woman may be, if truth and honesty are written across her face, she will be beautiful."

She knew it was Sidhant who had written this. Without losing her temper, Sara remarked, 'Oh! It seems some fellow has seriously started preparing for his MBA. If I'm not wrong, this is written by 'Roosevelt'. I don't remember his full name.'

A loud voice said, 'Eleanor Roosevelt'. It was Sidhant. No wonder he was three years senior but still sharing the same class with them. How could he be this big a fool - to confirm to Sara that what she thought was right?

Sara turned back and replied, 'Thanks for making me knowledgeable.'

At that moment, Sidhant realized what he had done. Sara was being sarcastic. It was a flop show for poor Sidhant. Meanwhile the professor entered the class and commenced his lecture. Someone in between had already cleaned up the board.

Anyways, Sidhant usually didn't come so early to the class for the lecture. After fifteen minutes, he started coughing and on that pretext moved out of the class, never to come back again.

It was June, time for completion of the second semester. Time had fled away fast. Sara was happy; her first year was about to end and only three years remained for completing graduation. She hadn't felt really comfortable in the college environment, and wanted to go back home as soon as possible. She viewed herself as more of a home bird than anything else.

Practical's started and in every course, Sara and Sidhant were often in the same group. When it came to studies Sara was damn serious, no Sidhant dared to disturb her focus.

She tried to help Sidhant in every practical, as she always found him standing disinterested, doing nothing. But every effort of hers was seemingly going down the drain as he was more interested in looking at his image in her eyes rather than paying heed to what she was saying.

Then examinations started. Each guy in the class except Sidhant, began circling around Sara and Avni for class notes. Now and then there used to be a call for them in the hostel, and someone was sitting in the guest room clearing his doubts. For Sidhant, this work was done for him by his stooges or might be, if he were the least bit interested in exams.

Avni received a phone call from Jimmy in the evening on Sunday. Last exam was scheduled for Monday and it was 'Thermodynamics', considered to be the toughest in their batch.

The boys decided to have a mass bunk, as nobody had prepared for the exam. Jimmy called up Avni to inform her regarding the same.

He said, 'Dear, you can understand, Saturday we were taking rest as the whole week gone by was extremely busy, and then on Sunday, the guys decided to watch 'Batman Begins'. It's a nice movie; you must also go with Sara one of these days to view it; so we couldn't prepare for the exam. I know you are extremely understanding. But make your eccentric friend also to think like a human being, and ask her to join the mass bunk. Please don't tell her whatever I have spoken about her. The truth is, everybody thinks the same way, and we have deep love for your flexible and friendly nature.'

After hearing Jimmy, Avni was on top of the world. She, in her mind even decided to suggest Sara to go and see the movie, next day, and make effective use of this break.

Avni knocked on Sara's door.

'Please come in.'

'Hi.' The room was full of loose papers scattered all around.

'It seems you are preparing hard for tomorrow's exam,' Avni said.

'Trying to, I need to maintain my grade point to qualify for scholarship.' Sara replied.

'But here's some twist to the story, ma'am. Some boys have decided for a mass bunk tomorrow as the poor things couldn't prepare for their exams. Jimmy called up and suggested we go to watch 'Batman Begins' tomorrow. It's a new release.'

Sara laid down on the bed, trying to focus on the book she held in her hands. Sara was patiently waiting for Avni to finish talking.

The moment Avni gave a pause, Sara's eyes pounced on Avni and she said, 'Who are boys to decide about tomorrow's exam? I spent two days preparing for it. Besides, everyone at home will be waiting for me. I already informed them that I would be immediately rushing for home as soon as exams are over. I'm feeling too stuffy here; I need to go back. I'm appearing for exam tomorrow in any case and I don't care even if I'm doing it alone'.

Avni, in her mind, was noting how correct the boys had been in their judgment of Sara's reaction. She thought, "They are so intelligent."

'What are you thinking, Avni? Do you want to come along with me? I'm sure you would have also done your preparations by now', Sara said.

'See Sara, I don't have any concerns on my preparations, however, I would like to maintain class unity. And the way you are worried about your GP, I think for sure, Jimmy would also be worried about it. I don't want to be a show spoiler for him and the others.'

'If he is so concerned about his GP, he shouldn't have gone to watch the movie. I hardly slept four hours last night because of stress and how could he afford to waste his two days like this?'

'Sara, you are from different planet, but we are human beings from this planet. We all desire to do things when we want.'

'Even if it is as important a thing as final exams? You can miss it to view a movie? What planet are you from?'

'Do whatever you want,' said Avni as she turned around to walk out of the room. 'I'll inform Jimmy about your decision.'

'It would be a great favor,' Sara yelled.

Both of them realized at that moment that it would be difficult for them to face each other, at least for a few days.

The boy's camp had anticipated that it wouldn't be easy to convince Sara for all the good reasons known to everybody, so they asked Jimmy to call up Avni again and confirm about Sara's reaction.

'Hi, Avni.'

'Jimmy, you guys were so right; she's so adamant. We had a big argument and she has refused to give up. I'm sure she'll be going for it, so manage her. I'm not going to appear as I have heretofore wasted too much time because of you people and I'm not prepared now.'

'You don't worry, we'll handle her tomorrow.'

Next day, Sara didn't wait for Avni to accompany her to the examination hall. Straight away she started marching towards it, half an hour before exam. She wanted to be there just in nick of time to avoid any controversies with her batch mates.

She got there at 9:15 a.m., fifteen minutes before the exam was set to start. As she entered the premises, to her surprise, she saw Avni already standing there along with the guys. Seeing Sara, they all scattered as mice do when sniffing a cat.

Boys are boys after all! They always have more arrows in their quivers.

This time it was Rohit, another classmate of Sara's. He was known to be handy with the girls. He knew how to change colors as per their mood swings. No, he wasn't a chameleon, but a very harmless guy who could make things run in any situation.

Sara was about to enter the examination hall. Someone called her from behind.

'Sara! Excuse me.'

'Hi.'

'I wanted to talk to you.'

'What is it Rohit?' she knew what he was about to say.

'Sara, please don't appear for the exam today, otherwise we all will automatically get an F grade. I know, our behavior was shameless. I apologize on behalf of everyone. We should have prepared for the exam, and especially since we knew it was the last. Can you understand that boys can be extremely careless when they are in mass?'

This last remark of Rohit's ruffled Sara's feathers.

'I'm not here to pay for the carelessness of you boys. I'm also not a psychiatrist to understand boy's behavior and their treatment.'

Rohit's expressions made it evident that while Sara was talking, he was preparing to take out another arrow. 'Sara, you are absolutely right in your reaction, but please tell me what's going to happen with Sidhant?'

'Sidhant! How did he come into the picture?'

'It's only he, we all are worried about. We can reappear in the exam and make it to the third semester. It shouldn't be an issue. But if Sidhant gets an 'F', this time he might even decide to leave engineering. You know, he has already wasted three years.'

'So rather than watching a movie he should have prepared for the exam.'

'No! He didn't go for the movie. On our request he didn't prepare; he slept in the hostel, he was not with us.'

Rohit was cognizant of the fact that he had confused Sara, and he could observe her getting a little softened.

The professor came out into the corridor, 'Please enter room number three for Thermodynamics. We are about to start the exam in another five minutes.'

No one moved. 'Sara, move in quickly,' the professor said.

Before she could say anything, Rohit came forward, 'Sir, we want this exam to be rescheduled as we couldn't prepare for it. It was not enough time.'

'Shut up, Rohit!' said their professor sternly. 'If you can't do it in two days than even the whole term would not be enough for you. I can't tolerate this drama. Go and talk to Dean. If it were me, I would simply give an 'F' to everyone.'

All the guys smiled. They knew the Dean would give them extra time.

What a misuse of student power.

It was a fun day and night in the boy's hostel. Every guy was coming to Sidhant's room to congratulate him. He was surprised, as he didn't have the faintest idea of what had happened at the examination hall. He was working diligently on the work assigned to him, 'Sleep'. When he was told, he thought they were just pulling his leg, so he brushed off the matter.

Jimmy knew it was all true and was not at all pleased with it.

Oh, Jimmy! How can he flirt with one and think about the other? It was true that Jimmy had always felt strongly for Sara and the reason he was with Avni was Sara. Jimmy spent time with Avni just to hear and know, more and more about Sara.

Finally, the exam was rescheduled and conducted and cleared by all. After exams there were the usual hugs, good-byes, exchange of wishes and all parted for a month long summer vacation.

CHAPTER 2

5 AUGUST, 2006: COLLEGE REOPENS. Sara and Avni were friends again and didn't even recall any incident before the holidays. Everyone was meeting with each other. Smiles were everywhere and there was an air of freshness and enthusiasm.

Sara saw Sidhant and said hello to him.

He smiled and replied, 'Hi'.

Sara felt very happy. At least he had learned how to respond back.

'Hey guys! It's party time again,' Rohit announced in the corridor. 'First three toppers of the past year, please contribute two months of scholarship. We are going to have a bash tomorrow.'

Sara, Jimmy and Avni knew they were going to be the host. No question of excuses as it was the college precedent.

So, next evening they had a party. Everyone was present except for Sidhant. Sara marked it, but made a conscious effort not to ask about him this time.

Afterwards, in the boy's hostel, there was a get together of the mechanical engineering guys. This was as per their ritual of assembling after every party or incident, either in the college or class.

Rohit said, 'Sidhant, something has happened to your market value. Today, Sara didn't show her concern for you. Probably, she has shifted her interests. She spent lot of time with Jimmy. I can recognize Jimmy's popularity index going up.'

'Hmmmm… '

Rohit was trying to test Sidhant's patience and instigate him against Sara. Sidhant could sense it out, but wasn't sure of the purpose.

'Hey! Rohit, you should be happy, she's going onto the right track. I know you are an exceptionally clean boy and always want the best for the girls, especially Sara.'

Both of them smirked. It was beyond the understanding of anyone else present in the room, on what conspired between these two guys. Fortunately the issue died right there.

College life went back to the usual routine.

A visit to a nearby car manufacturing plant was organized for second-year students as part of their curriculum. Jimmy was immensely excited as he would get some time to spend with the girls, and for that matter, so was everybody else. Sidhant had no interests in whatever happened.

Avni and Sara were also enthused, but for different reasons. 'I'm so happy, I'll experience one full day with Jimmy and that too without being captured in the CCTV cameras of the professor's eyes.'

'Oh God,' Sara said. 'I can't believe I'll be visiting a real manufacturing unit. My true journey as an engineer will begin that day. I hope the boys behave themselves and are serious about this trip. I'm very keen on going into every bit of the details there.'

Both girls clearly had different aspirations for the visit.

The day soon arrived, and the college bus was waiting outside the girl's hostel early in the morning around 5:00 a.m.

The bus beeped its horn for them and Avni and Sara came out at once, as they had been ready and waiting for some time.

Avni was dressed up, as if she was going for a party. She was wearing a denim mini skirt and pink top; thick mascara, deep eyeliner, pink lipstick and American diamond tops.

The door opened loudly. Avni entered the bus first. She climbed up the steps and every eye eagerly moved towards the door to see who was entering. Avni appeared with a big smile rotating her head to find a seat near Jimmy.

Avni was looking extremely beautiful and refreshing. The whole bus was cheerful at the sight of her.

Rohit was sitting with Jimmy and as soon as she saw him, Avni stared at Rohit as if suggesting him to go to hell. Rohit at once got up from there and sat on the only vacant seat, which was kept for girls.

Avni bounced onto the chair next to Jimmy, without realizing it was only vacated for her, so even if she takes a lifetime to reach there it would be lying vacant.

Next came in Sara. Surprisingly four eyes were on the door! Guess who? Rohit and Sidhant.

Sara looked boring beyond limits. A dull grey color suit, and white-colored sports shoes. She was dressed up as if she was wearing a uniform of some factory. Sara had no options but to sit beside Rohit.

'Good morning, how are you?' she asked.

'Good morning, I'm feeling much better after seeing you, Sara.'

Sara was taken aback by Rohit's flirtatious reply, but she chose to ignore it. At times she was very adjusting and realistic. She knew guys were in an excursion mood, so they were bound to do such silly things. She and Rohit started conversing with each other. Sara considered him a sensible guy and gave him due respect.

Sidhant as usual, spent his time staring at Sara, and this made, Rohit highly uncomfortable. Rohit smartly said, 'Sara come to the window seat, it's pleasant here.'

Sara could see as well, Sidhant doing whatever he was doing, so she too preferred to exchange seats with Rohit. Internally, she appreciated Rohit for his gesture. Sara was sure, he had done it to avoid the embarrassment Sidhant was causing her.

But, after few minutes, Sidhant came on the aisle side and continued what he was doing - staring at Sara.

It was expected to be a three hour journey. Around 8:30 a.m. they reached the factory.

They were standing in a queue outside the security gate as visitor's cards were being issued to them. With the formalities complete, the group assembled in a big veranda in front of the factory. The professor was giving them a list of Do's and Don'ts.

'Finally, you have to submit a visit report, so be attentive and take notes,' the professor said.

'Sure sir,' the group said in a chorus.

The mood was light. Avni was a treat for the eyes of everyone in the plant and she was feeling quite happy about it. Most of the guys in the group were eager, while Jimmy was somewhat indifferent. After all, he was Avni's "best friend".

Mr. Khan was introduced as the guide for the day. He was a senior manager in the production department. He was a very calm and composed man; perfect to handle the labor force.

He took them inside the plant, and started explaining about the assembly lines. Sara, Avni and Jimmy were the only three people really listening to Mr. Khan. Sara was also jotting down some notes. The rest of the guys were more interested in watching the girls, and how seriously Sara was behaving. Sidhant was amongst the group for around five minutes, and then he disappeared somewhere.

It was 12:30 p.m. Time for lunch break. Lunch was arranged in the plant mess where they were to have it with the workers and other staff members. As soon as the students reached the dining hall, the environment seemed to have got lightened. Instead of having serious discussions on the production schedule, everyone was sitting quiet, smiling. Avni was the center of attention.

Sara was unintentionally looking around for Sidhant. He didn't even turn up for lunch. From the mess window, she looked out to find Sidhant sitting outside in some shoddy canteen; smoking along with a few employees. Sara never liked this about Sidhant and always turned more negative toward him, after seeing his careless attitude.

Everyone was having lunch and Mr. Khan was impressed by Sara's seriousness and intelligence. He started talking to her about her experiences so far, her interests and many other things.

Meanwhile, Sidhant entered the hall and looked around for the group. He came closer to Sara and found Mr. Khan chatting with her. This made him uneasy, and it was evident on his face. He sat beside Rohit and took just five minutes to eat his food and then leave the mess.

The group of students resumed their tour from one department to another. Then, before they knew it, it was 4:30 p.m.; time to depart.

Mr. Khan gave his e-mail id and phone number to the group and assured them of every help they might require in completing their reports. Visitor's passes were returned at the security gate and everyone boarded the bus. Sidhant was still missing, but before the professor could identify that he was absent, he arrived at the bus.

On the drive back, everyone was tired and that morning's cheer was absent.

8:30 p.m.: The girls were dropped at their hostel and the bus moved towards the boy's hostel.

During this journey, Sara and Rohit became very friendly and she fancied him as a good person.

As per the norm, the guys were to have a get together but they decided to postpone it to the next day.

Next day: The 'trip' was the point of discussion in the college. The seniors were curious to know more about the two girls and any other interesting occurrences.

'Hey Sara,' Rohit said when he saw her later on campus. 'You are still looking tired. Let's go to the canteen and have a cup of tea.'

Sara didn't feel that she looked tired but accompanied Rohit. When they reached the canteen, Sara noticed Sidhant sitting there. Sidhant was glaring at Sara.

Sara tried to ignore his staring and focused on Rohit. Rohit had a lot to say and Sara appeared to be paying attention to Rohit, but her mind wasn't there. They finished their tea and moved back towards the college. Sidhant kept sitting there, puffing at his cigarette.

In the evening, it was the time for the boy's meeting. Avni was the hot topic. Lots of loose comments were passed. Jimmy kept quiet and showed his indifference. Then Sara became the focus.

From somewhere Sidhant's voice came, 'Okay Rohit, let's talk about Sara. Yesterday, she sat with you for a full six hours. How did she smell?' It seemed Sidhant wanted to utter a lot of filth.

God knows why. Perhaps, it was nothing against Sara, but he wanted to find out Rohit's reaction.

Mr. Cool, known for his patience and negotiations couldn't maintain his calm. He rebuffed Sidhant and threatened to slap him if he even uttered a single more word about Sara. It got very tense. Some of the boys had to come in between to pacify the whole situation. The whole scene got nasty.

Sidhant was very upset at Rohit's behavior and didn't sleep well that night, which was unlike Sidhant. He didn't realize it, but he was getting possessive about Sara. Now finding Rohit and Sara getting closer to each other, Sidhant got disturbed and wanted to know the truth.

He decided he would convince Rohit to get this clarity from Sara.

Next day, Rohit and Sara were again seen together at the canteen. Rohit was joyful about it. Rohit started discussing the previous night's episode.

'Sidhant was saying something about you last night.'

Sara couldn't hide her curiosity, 'What was that?'

'Sorry, that I can't tell you as you would be offended. Moreover, he was drunk so no point deliberating over what he was trying to say.'

'Disgusting! I used to consider him a nice guy, but he's just a flicker.'

Rohit took this as an opportunity and added, 'Nice! He's a very cheap guy; I have never seen him respecting females. He invariably talks rubbish about them and demeans them.'

Sara was hurt. Even Rohit could make it out from her face, which turned red. 'Let's go back to the college,' Sara said. 'I'm getting queasy. Maybe, I would like to go to the hostel.'

Jimmy also spoke to Avni and told him the things almost on the same line.

There's an old saying, "Where there is smoke there is fire". In reality, it wasn't Sidhant who wanted clarity on anyone's feelings rather it was vice versa. Everyone, especially Rohit and Jimmy could always see that smoke in Sara and Sidhant's restlessness, so they wanted to know the truth of the fire. At least for his part, Rohit wanted to quench it as soon as possible. Both of them were giving an effort towards that end.

The irony was, except for Sidhant and Sara, everyone could identify the fire.

Sara came back early from the college that day. In the evening, she heard Avni calling her. 'Sara, where are you?'

'What happened?' Sara said in a little meek tone.

'You know, Sidhant is so vulgar. Last night he created a scene about you in the boy's hostel.'

Without listening to rest of the sentence, Sara replied, 'Yes, I heard about it'.

'Who told you?'

'Rohit'

Avni was pacified to find Rohit at least being a support to Sara.

Sara projected her calm. And without even revealing to her the reason for her meek tone and ill health said, 'It happens! Guys cross their limits and they don't realize it. Maybe it happened with Sidhant too. Moreover, he was drunk. Let's leave it and discuss something else.'

'How was your day? Oh, can you give me all the notes for the lectures I have missed today?' Sara asked.

'Ok sure, take some rest for now,' Avni said moving out of Sara's room.

At times, girls are too simple. Avni wanted to cry for Sara without knowing that what was uttered for her last night, if it was told to her, she would never go back to college again.

Sara was wondering, "I want to hate Sidhant for everything, he's cheap, a drunkard, callous... then also I'm unable to abhor him, and I'm even trying to defend him in front of others."

Unable to understand her behavior and finding herself helpless, she bolted her room from inside and started weeping. She was never this kind before, who would sob for something like a guy, and that too, someone like Sidhant.

She felt better after crying; she came out of the room, and started chatting with the girls standing there.

For his part, Sidhant was also feeling fidgety. No clue why? He decided to talk to Rohit.

'Hi buddy, I'm sorry for yesterday. I know you like Sara, and it was wrong on my part to talk loosely about her.'

This was totally unexpected from Sidhant. Rohit felt really encouraged to hear those words from him and his direct acknowledgment of the fact that he liked Sara.

It was now Rohit's turn to console Sidhant. 'No worries! It happens at times. There's something more, which is really disturbing me.'

'What?'

'Jimmy has told everything to Avni and you know Avni...'

'Do you think she told it to Sara in the college itself?'

'Yep', Rohit nodded. It was too Machiavellian on Rohit's part.

'Was that the reason for Sara leaving early today?' Sidhant was curious to know.

'Possibly, yes,' Rohit said.

Sidhant felt like slapping himself for that. Finally he moved out of Rohit's room.

Rohit could feel butterflies in his stomach. He was too anxious to meet Sara the next day.

He thought it was a race; whoever takes the lead wins.

Next day in the college:

'How are you feeling today?' Rohit asked Sara.

'Good, thanks.'

'Let's go to the canteen, we'll talk for some time.'

'Is it important?'

'No, only if you like. Sara you look down today, so I thought maybe it'll help.'

Sara couldn't say no to his concern and followed Rohit to the canteen. He felt more confident that day, everything seemed under his control.

The moment they reached there; she noticed Sidhant as usual, and he couldn't keep himself from staring at her.

Rohit was thinking, "Shameless! He knows there's something between us, why can't he leave us alone for some time?"

'Sara, should we go to some other place?'

'Why?'

'Maybe the presence of this brazen creature is disturbing you,' he said nodding in the direction of Sidhant.

'Why should he disturb me?' Sara couldn't hear anything against Sidhant, but internally she was always annoyed with him.

'Okay as you wish, you sit and forget about everything. I want you to relax and chat with me.'

Sara raised her brows and thought, "Who's he to want something for me, he's acting too funny!"

'Sara, what do you think about me?'

Girls have a sixth sense and this time, this sense was telling Sara that something stupid was coming from Rohit.

'You are a nice, friendly guy but at times, you act over smart. If you can mend this trait of yours and try to mind your own business, you can be a better person'.

This came as a blow to Rohit, who was expecting at least something soft, if not romantic from Sara. Without losing his confidence he continued, 'Do you like me?'

Sara knew for sure now, where he is leading to. 'I don't think there's much in you to be disliked.'

Sara was doing her best to stop Rohit from saying anything awkward. She never wanted to lose a good associate.

Rohit without getting discouraged said, 'It's a fact, I like you.'

'What do you mean?'

'I like you and want to be friends forever.'

'How absurd!' Sara stood up from the bench.

'Please sit, everyone around us is looking here.'

Sara calmed herself and sat down, 'Rohit, we hardly know each other! Moreover it's only our second year and how can you have such weird ideas? You boys are so myopic in your thinking. It's just, I talked to you nicely few times and came to canteen with you, and suddenly you thought something is brewing between us!'

'No! No! Sara, I genuinely like you, and thought I will share my feelings with you.'

'You need to manage yourself; just because we live in a democratic country doesn't mean you take a box of likings in your hand and start distributing it on the road,' Sara was losing her temper. 'How can you hurt my feelings in this way because you considered something?'

Rohit turned red now, not with anger but due to fear; he was sure he would be exposed in the college and was going to be a laughingstock for several days to come. He felt as if he was losing everything and in desperation said, 'Sara, I'm sorry if I have hurt you, but my intentions were true and I said whatever I felt. You are right, it was one sided, and I had no indications from your end. I request that you forget this and be your original self.'

She looked away towards some trees in the distance. 'It's not easy; I'll try my best to ignore it but no promises.'

She left the canteen and everyone sitting there could smell something wrong had happened. Sidhant on the other hand felt he knew what had taken place. He anticipated something like this happening any day and was keeping his fingers crossed over Sara's reaction. Now, he had gained some clarity.

'Shot, shot...one gone'. He smiled. He stood up from there and followed Sara to the class.

Things started moving as usual. Sara didn't mention anything to anyone. Rohit also didn't talk about it, yet he had a notion that Sidhant knew everything. In fact, from core of his heart he was blaming Sidhant for this fiasco. He was the one who gave him this confidence and misled him.

For a few days, Sara came to college but turned a blind eye to Rohit. She didn't even say 'hello'. Eventually they got back to normal and there were no hard feelings. Sara was more comfortable with him now. Perhaps, it was because Rohit now had an idea about her feelings and there was no confusion between them. She felt bad for Rohit, but she knew it's easier for boys to forget and cope with such issues. As per Sara's perceptions, boys like Rohit were street Romeo's; they can't stick to one girl and for them life never stops.

Sara even started confiding in him issues regarding Sidhant or anything else which disturbed her. Rohit was proving to be a sincere friend.

October arrived and it was time to start contemplating giving a welcome party to the freshers. Rohit called for a class meeting in the college garden on the fifth of October at around 5:00 p.m.

Avni and Sara came back from college that day excited as the day was a bit relaxed. There was no practical or workshop in the afternoon. Avni was hungry, so straight away they headed to the hostel canteen. They ordered their favorite food - bread omelet for Avni and 'Maggi' noodles, boiled with no vegetables for Sara.

They were mingling with the rest of the girls, which was a rare scene as they were usually too busy with their daily routine, especially Sara who was a noted bookworm.

Someone told them that Juhi, who had joined the electrical stream that year, was sick, and their mechanical seniors had gone to her room to see her.

Sara became concerned, and she suggested Avni and she join the rest of the girls and ask about Juhi's welfare.

The group of girls went to her room. Sara and Avni were meeting her for the first time. She was a cute girl but was looking frail.

Sara was a very compassionate girl and always loved the positive side of human nature. She got very friendly with Juhi in a minute, and Juhi also felt comfortable with her. After half an hour, all the girls in the room decided to leave so that Juhi could rest; Sara volunteered to take care of her while she slept.

Juhi fell asleep as soon as the girls went away. Sara could see that she was uneasy all the time and wasn't having a sound sleep.

'Do you need something, Juhi?'

'Gimme some water, Sara.'

Sara gave her water and then fresh juice.

Suddenly, she started throwing up and had to be rushed to the campus hospital. Sara accompanied her to the hospital. The doctor said there was no major cause of worry. It was a case of mild food poisoning. He put her down on drip, gave one injection of ondem to stop vomiting and a few antibiotics to control her infection. They kept her in the hospital for a night under observation. Sara stayed with her.

The next morning, she was discharged from the hospital and meanwhile her parents had also arrived there. They took her back to their hometown till she fully recovered.

Sara came back to the hostel, and took two hours of sleep. She felt fresh, got ready and went to the college along with Avni.

Everyone became surprised to see her at classes. One senior approached her and said, 'Are you okay now? We heard you were in the hospital yesterday. What happened?'

'No! No! It was not me; It was Juhi, first year electrical student.'

'How's she now?'

'Her parents have taken her back home. She was better; she got discharged in the morning.'

'Oh.'

Rohit, Jimmy, and everyone else came rushing to Sara, asking the same set of questions. Even Sidhant came from behind. He didn't say a word but his eyes were showing his anxiety.

Sara got a very warm feeling about her classmates and how much they cared for her.

She left early for the hostel that day and Rohit walked her there.

It being a weekend; she planned to go home. Going home was always a pleasure; eat and sleep, there's nothing much to do. Family doesn't expect you to do much as you are home only for a few hours. Everyone tries to pamper you.

Sara was from a rich traditional family. They were traditional but not conservative. They wanted the girls to be educated and independent. Her mother was a doctor, and she wanted her to do something which gave her satisfaction and never tried to impose anything upon her.

Sara never desired to be a doctor as she wanted to do something challenging. She was like a tom boy in her early days. The reason she chose mechanical engineering was that it gave her a macho feeling, very similar to what Sidhant considered, which was distinct from a stereotypical girl.

Sara was brought up in a small nuclear family. She had a younger sister, Diya, who was four years younger than her. It was a close-knit family. As compared to her mother, her father was a strict man.

Some things were never discussed at home, but were mandated. Limits need to be strictly maintained with the opposite sex. No act of yours should reflect any cheapness. Her family created lot of fuss over ethics and morality. Marriage shouldn't be the ultimate aim for anyone, it happens in due time.

The prime duty of kids is to first attain good education, be good human beings and become self-sufficient.

Sara's parents were neither too ambitious nor had they taught their kids to be that way. They had always given importance to good human values.

Monday, 5th October: It was time for Sara to go back. When you are at home time flies by.

Sara took the early morning train and reached the hostel at around 9:30 a.m. First lecture would have already started, so she thought there was no point in rushing to the college.

She took some rest, had a cup of tea, and listened to her favorite music. Sara was fond of classical music, unlike others of her generation.

At 11:00 a.m. she started for the college to join the class for second lecture. When she reached there she saw most of her class coming from the canteen. Sidhant was also part of the group. She became hopeful of the professor being absent that day.

'What happened, you guys didn't attend the class?'

'No point, when the scholar's not there we aren't interested. It's just to give *you* company that we sit in the class.' Except for Rohit, no one could have dared to say this to Sara.

'Okay guys!' said Rohit. 'Don't forget we are meeting today at 5:30 p.m., in the garden.'

At the appointed time everyone was gathered there. The agenda for the welcome party was being discussed.

'It will start with a welcome speech, dance item, skit, anything fresher's shall be interested in, time slot of maximum 10 minutes would be allotted to them and eventually the vote of thanks by freshers,' Rohit announced.

'I'll go there to have drinks and an elaborate dinner,' Jimmy said.

'We know, in fact most of us will! What do you say Sidhant?' Rohit looked at him.

He just smiled. Sidhant never became party to any kind of low level discussions. Most of the time, he was quiet and maintained his grace. At times he became a bit harsh and sarcastic, but never cheap.

'We'll have drinks followed by dinner,' Rohit said vociferously.

'There will be around 100 people, so each need to contribute 1000 bucks, but that will also not suffice. We also need to get a little sponsorship and we should target a collection of Rs 25,000-30,000 from that. In case of any further shortfalls, we will find out some means.

'As decided, let's keep it tentatively for 1st Nov. I will try to ask Dean Sir for his approval and check for his availability.

'Sara, Avni, Rohit, Jimmy and Sidhant are part of the collection team and shall update you with the status after ten days. So we are meeting after ten days at the same time and place. Thank you, guys.'

'Hoooooooo thank you, Rohit!'

Every year almost the same procedure was followed. There was a list of companies with the seniors, who contributed last year to their fund, so they just had to go to them and ask for more funds. As the economy was booming those days corporates were a bit more generous in contributing.

When they met after ten days they had already collected Rs 20,000 and preparations were going forward smoothly.

Rohit asked Sara to take part in the dance item to which she refused, so it was decided she would give the welcome speech and Avni would participate in dance item. He also asked Sara to help the boys with their makeup.

Avni started giggling. She knew how bad Sara was at these things, but Sara gave her a disapproving look.

Sidhant was looking at Sara and concluded that she was too rigid and short tempered in her behavior.

The only topic discussed those days in the college was the 'freshers party'. After every lecture, second year mechanical batch was deliberating in the corridor on some new issue. Everything was under their control and it was their first occasion to show their administrative and creative skills.

Rohit knew a choreographer, and he was helping the boys in preparing the dance item. Like everyone else, Avni was also enjoying her part.

The skit portrayed certain interesting incidents which happened during ragging, and Sara too was offered a small role in it. In fact, it wasn't a role but the character she actually was at the time of ragging - a compassionate, protective senior somewhat like a big sister. In the beginning, she thought the guys were pulling her leg. But she was never the kind of person who ran away from reality, and the fact was 'yes', she acted like a big sister during ragging period so the guys were trying to have fun now. She agreed to play her part.

In total, they collected Rs 35,000 from corporate sponsorships and individuals, which were more than any other year gone by.

Every day they would have practice sessions. Avni was a good dancer, so she was the highlight of the dance. The rest of the boys, were average in their dancing skills. It was only Sidhant whose dancing movements were so awkward that at times the choreographer yelled at him, 'Sir, why you are testing my patience?' Sara enjoyed watching the dance item.

Except for Sara, everyone had a hunch that Sidhant's regular appearance at the practice sessions was only because he wanted to be around Sara more. Everyone thought he was a flirt, and was trying to tease Sara.

It was the final day, freshers party day. The sequence of the activities planned for the evening was as follows:

- Welcome address by Sara
- Dance item by second-year students
- Skit by second-year students
- Classical dance performance by first-year students
- Vote of thanks by first-year students
- Drinks and dinner

Since morning, everyone was busy doing their part. Sara had the least to do. She came dressed up from the hostel. Then she was to help guys in their makeup for the skit and, she herself was to play her role in the same attire.

The stage was set for the show. It was a huge hall. Guests were seated in time.

A voice came from microphone. 'Hello, hello. It's working fine, I can continue. Life is all about aspirations, and today we are here because we perceive our alma mater is the road towards our life! Good evening everyone and a heartiest welcome to all the new, enthusiastic and pretty faces.'

Everyone was stunned to see this amazing young lady in a sea blue sari, nicely tucked; sleeveless blouse, green and blue stone necklace around her neck, attractively done shoulder length hair and long pencil heels. Slim and tall, she was looking gorgeous. Her face was glowing and her bold dark eyes were catching attention.

There was hardly anyone listening to what she said!

As soon as she came on the stage and started speaking, there was a storm in the dressing room. The whole group was trying to peep out to see Sara.

A voice said, 'Sidhant, Sara out there'. Sidhant straight away came on the window from where the view was clear.

Sidhant jumped off the window, saying, 'Anyways, I'm not interested in dancing.' He occupied the corner last seat in the hall and started gazing at Sara.

The way he jumped off the window, and came inside the hall, caught Sara's attention too. She had an eye-to-eye contact with him for a while. However, she regained her focus and continued with her address. 'So I, on behalf of all the seniors, would like to welcome you to this prestigious college. I hope you have the time of your lives. Thank you.'

A hearty round of applause echoed in the hall.

Rohit took over the microphone from Sara. 'Thanks Sara. Moby once said, "Scotland is one of my favorite places to perform; it's really something special. Scottish audiences are just so enthusiastic; their approach to dance music just feels similar to my own somehow," So the onus is now on you audience! Let's see whether we can make this place feel like Scotland or not, for our Moby's.'

The audience laughed.

While Rohit was engaged with the audience, Jimmy and the others came from behind and dragged Sidhant back into the dressing room. Sidhant felt embarrassed at this gesture, but quickly got ready for his action.

The curtains were raised and the guys and Avni started their dance item. Avni was stealing the show, and so the guys were trying to do their best as well.

'Hoooooooooooo hoooooooooooo'; the audience truly made it a Scotland. All freshers were standing, dancing and hooting. Why not? After so many months they were getting back their freedom.

Next event was fresher's show. They had to perform a classical dance. As they were performing their dance, Sara was in the dressing room helping the guys with their makeup and hair. Then it was Sidhant's turn, and the coordinator told Sara to tie a ponytail for him. Sidhant had shoulder length hair, and he used to loosely put a band around it. But as he was imitating Professor Sanskriti he was required to tie it in a ponytail. It was absurd for Sara. However she couldn't dare to say 'no'. She took his hair in her hand, but they just slipped away as they were so silky. She was really struggling to raise them and tie a band.

Time was running by, as the skit was the next item. As much as Sara was trying to hurry up, the more things were landing in a mess. Sidhant was enjoying this time for two reasons: He had never seen Sara doing something so patiently and second he could feel the soothing touch of her silky hands which was making him feel out of this world. The guys around them were also having a nice time as they have never seen either of them like this. Lastly, she could tie a crippled ponytail, somewhat shabbily done.

Sidhant turned around, smiled and asked, 'Done?'

'Yep.'

Finally they were on the stage. It was a humorous skit. Everyone, including Sara was enjoying doing and watching it.

As soon as the program was over, Jimmy rushed towards Sara.

'You are looking gorgeous!'

Sara smiled and replied, 'Thank you, but it's all in your eyes. Besides, everyone is looking great tonight, don't you think?'

Jimmy smiled and nodded in agreement.

Sidhant had overheard Jimmy's remark and didn't feel good about it.

The evening ended with dinner and Sara was the highlight of the day.

CHAPTER 3

TILL NOW IT WAS fun and frolic on campus, even the professors were going slow. After fresher's party though, the educational tempo built up, for the second and first year students to finish their courses.

The months passed and it was time for end of the session. Second-year students started preparing for one month summer training. Companies came for campus interviews, and some guys opted for their personal engagements.

Jimmy and Sara got selected together to an automobile ancillary company; Avni and Sidhant got through to a capital equipment company. They all had to go to Bangalore for their training.

Jimmy was excited with the idea of spending a full month with Sara. Sara was calm although bit uneasy. She felt emotionally sick. She was a typical Indian girl, too attached with her family. Avni was upset because she wouldn't be with Jimmy for a month. And for Sidhant, Avni was more of a girlish girl; less intellect more femininity. Sidhant dreaded such a combination.

The session finished on 27th May. Summer training was scheduled to start on 1st June. There was no time for anyone to spend with their families. Some guys preferred to go directly to their training stations without taking a halt at their home. However, Sara immediately rushed to her home in Delhi.

She was booked for Bangalore Rajdhani Express on 29th May, from Hazrat Nizamuddin Railway station, Delhi. Jimmy also joined her at the station and together they started their journey, which was to be around 36 hours long.

Sidhant and Avni were from Mumbai, so they were also travelling together.

Sara and Jimmy started gossiping the moment they entered the train.

Professor Malik, Sanskriti ma'am.... every professor was discussed on the way; their qualifications, even their families were also discussed.

'Sara, you know Professor Gupta's daughter is in Campus school X standard, and Sidhant is flirting with her.'

It changed the course of conversation. Sara became a little stiff. She wondered why he had brought it up. 'He seems to be a big feral creature; you keep hearing such things about him now and then,' Sara remarked.

Sara neither had control over her tongue nor her anger. What if Jimmy, repeats it to Sidhant? After all, they were good friends. Sara, in impulse, always did something which might hurt Sidhant, and then at a second thought always repented her gesture.

Sidhant and Avni were sitting quietly on their train. After every ten or fifteen minutes, Avni took out a face mirror from her hand bag and did a retouch of her makeup. Sidhant looked at her stoically. Sidhant was engrossed in his novel '*Sense and Sensibility*' by Jane Austen. All of a sudden he said, 'Avni, how much do you spend on your cosmetics in a month?'

'Around Rs 10,000'

'Who pays for it?'

'My parents'

'What if you get married tomorrow and your hubby can't afford it?'

'Talk sense, Sidhant! I'm good looking, from a rich family; why would I marry a pauper? By the way, I have never found you so analytical in class. It's better you learn to have a self-focus, otherwise you'll waste half of the time in analyzing hypothetical things.' She was certainly irked by his comment.

Sidhant realized that, Avni hadn't taken his remark in a good light. He thought, it'd be better to concentrate on his book.

Later, Avni was sleeping. Dinner was being served in the train. Sidhant decided not to take the dinner and asked them to keep it in the kitchen.

'We'll ask for it when she gets up.'

'Sir, should I keep it for you?'

'Nope, keep both the plates in the kitchen.'

After half an hour or so Avni got up from her sleep and saw littered plates lying on the sides of the floor.

'Oh I have missed my dinner. You should have woken me up.'

Sidhant got up from his berth, went into the kitchen and picked up the two plates.

'Here's your food, you haven't missed anything.'

Avni immediately came on the lower berth feeling embarrassed about her reaction. She felt good about this thoughtful action by Sidhant. They finished their dinner and Avni again went to sleep while Sidhant resumed reading his novel.

Avni got up early in the morning. She was afraid of standing in the queue for the toilet. She quickly grabbed one for her. When she came out, there was a long line outside the lavatory. No wonder she dreaded queues, she knew how people can test someone's patience. Makeup took her long as washroom was a small place in the train. When she came out, people looked at her with hostile eyes.

'Oops sorry!' she rushed back to her berth. Sidhant slept meanwhile.

Breakfast and lunch was served. Avni asked them to keep the food in the kitchenette for them. Sidhant was still in slumber.

The train was about to arrive and Sidhant was still wandering in his dreamland.

'Wake up Sidhant, wake up!'

'Let me sleep, I don't want breakfast.'

'Breakfast, lunch everything is there in the kitchen, but there's no time left to eat it. We are arriving in another five minutes.'

'Oh God!' He jumped from his berth, packed his bags, put on his shoes and got ready to go.

Avni gave him a sour look.

'What?'

'You haven't even brushed your teeth.'

'It's ok; I'll do it in the guest house.'

The train stopped. They reached Bangalore and hired a cab to go straight to the guest house. Avni felt so uncomfortable in the cab. It was foul smelling because of Sidhant.

Sidhant thought, "Oh God! She's going to make my life hell by making these crazy faces. I'll have to take a bath daily."

Finally, they arrived at the guest house located in 'Indranagar', a nice posh locality.

Jimmy and Sara were still on the train with some time to go. Sara was reading her book 'A Walk To Remember', by Nicholas Sparks. Jimmy was sleeping and at times staring at Sara to catch her attention. Contrary to his expectations, it was a boring journey.

Ultimately, they reached Bangalore and their guest house was in Jayanagar. They hired a cab and the first thing Sara asked the driver, 'How far is Indranagar from Jayanagar?'

'Ma'am, it shall take you around 35 minutes in this traffic.'

'Oh it's nearby! How's this place Jayanagar?'

'It's one of the oldest and well established areas in the city. It's a simple and conservative locality.'

'Oh!'

Jimmy asked with curiosity that if there were some theaters around there.

'Yes there are five of them in that area. INOX, shanthi cinemas...'

'Good!'

'We can go and meet Avni on one of these days,' Sara said.

Jimmy was not thrilled with the idea. He wanted to spend some time alone with Sara.

'Yes, of course, we'll get a chance to meet Sidhant too.'

'Who cares?'

There was as a smile on Jimmy's face, 'Whatever you say.'

'No definitely, we'll go and meet them,' Sara said.

Avni was anxiously waiting for Jimmy to reach his guest house. By the time he reached there, she had called about ten times.

***

At the reception desk, 'It's Jimmy, we have come here for summer training.'

'Oh, you are Jimmy! Avni rang up several times; I think it's something urgent. You must call her without delay.'

'Sure, thanks.'

Sara smiled. Jimmy felt embarrassed. They moved into their respective rooms.

Jimmy rushed to call Avni. 'How are you?'

'Eager to talk to you.'

'I came to know that. You called up a lot of times at my guest house.'

'Yep.'

'How's everything at your end? How's Sidhant?'

'Eek! This man is so filthy and boring.'

'Hahaaaa……..

'How did he behave during the journey?'

'I was amazed to find out a new shade of his personality-he is too caring,' Jimmy wasn't pleased to hear it.

'Did he talk about Sara?'

'No, even he didn't mention her name once.'

'Wonderful!'

'Why are you getting so happy?'

'I'm happy for Sara. At least, he has stopped saying filth about her. After all, she is a good friend,' Jimmy said twisting the conversation.

'Let's leave Sara; tell me, "Are you missing me?"'

'Avni dear, I was only thinking about you throughout my journey. I wish, instead of Sara you were with me. She is such a dull person.' Avni was on cloud nine after hearing Rohit and wished if she could immediately fly to him.

'Rohit, you can't imagine- how much did I miss you.'

'Avni, it's too late; I feel you must sleep now.'

'Okay, Good Night. Let's catch up tomorrow.'

'Good Night'

'Bye.'

Jimmy went to Sara's room. It seemed to be locked from inside. He knocked twice but no one came to open the door. Jimmy assumed Sara was catnapping as she didn't sleep for the last two days because she was involved in reading her book. He went back to his room, switched on the TV, and browsed from one channel to another until finally he fell asleep.

Jimmy and Sara met at the breakfast table, disposed to start their day with lots of optimism. If you prove yourself, there's a good chance of getting recruited in these corporations.

Jimmy and Sara; Avni and Sidhant, reached their respective destinations early in order to make good first impressions. The day passed by. They were briefed about the training agenda and introduced to the instructors of the various departments. Visits to the plant were organized. Sidhant happily realized that he would get ample time to chill out.

A few days later, Sidhant asked Avni if she would like to go out with him to his cousin's house, who stayed nearby. Avni got enthused by the idea.

They reached Shonit's house at around 4:00 p.m. His wife, Divya, was stunning. They had a one-year-old daughter, a cute baby. She was coughing a lot. Sidhant asked Divya, 'What has happened to her?' She told him it was allergic bronchitis. She started grumbling about Shonit being a chain smoker and aggravating the baby's illness.

Sidhant got a little piqued, he remarked, 'Shonit you should stop that immediately! Look at the kid, she is suffering a lot.'

'You are right bro. I'm trying my best, but this work pressure drags me back to it.'

'It's farcical Shonit! You should set your priorities right.'

Divya said, 'Almost every day we have a fight over this issue, but he's unable to control himself.'

'Ok Divya, leave it for now. Sidhant has come after such a long time.'

Shonit told Avni, 'Sorry, I missed your name.'

'Hi, I'm Avni.'

'You are friends?'

Before Avni could say anything, Sidhant said, 'Nope, we are just classmates.'

Shonit and Divya were very nice, cheerful people. Avni enjoyed their company. As they were getting ready to leave, Divya presented a perfume to Avni.

'Thanks, that's not required.'

'It's ok; you have come to our home for the first time.'

'Keep it Avni.' Sidhant said. Avni liked the authority in his voice.

They came back to their guest house and Avni could not stop herself from calling Jimmy.

'Hi Jimmy.'

'Is everything ok? You are calling so late.' Avni told him everything about the day.

Jimmy was happy, as he thought Avni and Sidhant were getting closer.

Jimmy always considered Avni as his very good friend. He was protective about her but not possessive; whereas he knew Avni took him in a very different light and was emotional about him. They didn't share the same feelings.

Jimmy was having a rather dull routine with Sara. Sara was taking her training too seriously, and the remaining time she preferred to spend with her books. Jimmy had proposed for a movie to Sara, but she denied as she wasn't willing to move out anywhere.

Sidhant and Avni were having good time. Elbow greasing at the plant, and jotting notes was Avni's portfolio; excursions and fun time was designed by Sidhant. But Avni extended her full support to him.

Ultimately, four of them planned to go for a movie on last weekend at Bangalore, and fortunately this time, Sara didn't resist. Avni was thrilled to meet Jimmy after a long time. Girls sat in the middle escorted by the guys on two sides. Sidhant was different, not protective about girls but he didn't have any choice as Sara opted to sit with Avni, Avni was with Jimmy so he had to settle with Sara on the other end. Sara and Sidhant just greeted each other and didn't utter even a single word after that.

Sidhant could hear Sara sobbing in between on any emotional scene. It surprised him to find Sara so sentimental; she looked like an aggressive and strong girl. Sidhant being a light hearted boy or supposedly so, as he showcased himself like that, thought of enjoying this situation. Next time, any tear jerking scene came up, even before waiting for Sara to voice any beeps, he handed over a tissue to her. Unconsciously she took it in her hand than when she realized what it was, she screamed, ' I don't need one, and did I ask for it?'

'Oh sorry, I thought you might need it'

'No, thanks!'

Sidhant enjoyed it. He was childish at times.

They had dinner after the movie, and then moved back to their destinations.

Avni enjoyed her time with Jimmy. Jimmy seemed amused, but Sara was upset on Sidhant's puerile act.

'Leave it Sara, don't spoil your mood. You are aware of his behavior.'

'You are right, Jimmy.'

Jimmy thought, "It's propitious time to get heart to heart with Sara, as she's opening up with him."

'Sara do you find any distinction between me and Sidhant?'

'Ha! How can you compare an apple with a banana?'

'Who's apple?'

'Of course, it's you!' Sara casually remarked.

'And you like apples'

Sara paused and looked at him........

'No, the reason I'm asking this is that I like both'

Sara, now, became conscious of what was coming, 'I don't like fruits'

Jimmy thought of coming straight away to the point, 'Sara you might not like me but I really feel good about you'

'Who stops you? It's great you feel good about me!'

'I mean, I love you not only for what you are; but for what I am, when I am with you.'

'Love! Excuse me..........'

'We are merely acquainted with each other and moreover, you are with Avni.

'How dare you manipulate two girls like this?

'Avni will be shocked to know it. She likes you so much, and you have been equally involved with her.'

'Sara, we are just friends.'

'Shut up Jimmy! How can you be so insensitive?

'Anyways, it's your personal matter with Avni, I'm no one.

'I'm finding it bizarre that you have proposed me out of blue, let me make it absolutely clear to you that you are just a friend and nothing more than that.'

There was a lull between them till the time they reached back.

At the guest house Jimmy said, 'Good night, Sara,' without saying anything she moved to her room.

Sara was restless that night. She wondered, "Why this is happening with me? I haven't been overly friendly with anyone in the class or college then why people are getting these wrong impressions?"

Suddenly it came to her mind, "Is it Sidhant behind this mess? Is he making fun of me or trying to belittle these guys at my cost?" She had an immensely bad taste in her mouth, when she thought about it.

Next morning, Sara sat on the breakfast table; Jimmy joined her, he looked a little low.

'Good morning,' Sara neither looked up nor replied.

'Sara, I'm really sorry if I have hurt you in any way'

'No, you haven't only hurt me, but have also cheated Avni'

'That's wrong; I and Avni are just good friends. I haven't said anything to her beyond that.

'You can ask her if you don't believe me'

'You understand she's crazy for you'

'Yes I know, it's entirely my fault but can I request you something?'

'What?'

'Please don't tell it to Avni; otherwise, she would crack'

'You guys are so treacherous'

CHAPTER 4

*7*HEY FINISHED THEIR TRAINING and departed back to their homes. Sara hasn't expected such an ironical end to her training, and Avni had never imagined that he would find a good friend in Sidhant. Jimmy's ambitions were shattered, and Sidhant was glad to identify- how easy it was to handle the girls. Each of them had mixed feelings.

Everything apart, the biggest fact was, they had been promoted to the next year.

Next session started in mid-July, everyone came back from their trainings and homes. Campus placements were good that year; almost an increase of 10-25% in packages was offered from the last session. Half of the students opted to pursue higher studies. Everywhere there was a wave of MBA. Guys were preparing for CAT and wanted to qualify for IIM's. A few graduates thought of going abroad for pursuing higher studies. Guys started focusing on their preparations from third year onwards. Sara, also, before coming back to college had enrolled for ' IMS tutorials'. They used to be considered as good for MBA preparation.

First day in the college; The whole class asked first three toppers to shell out their two month scholarship for class party. As usual Sara, Avni and Jimmy have to part off with their money.

This time the party was organized at 'Dawat' restaurant. Rohit organized it. He had become a seasoned player by then. Program was drinks followed by dinner.

On the party day, two hosts Sara and Avni arrived at the venue a little earlier then the scheduled time. Sidhant was the only guy who had reached by that time. "Perhaps, drinks pulled him there or was it Avni?" Sara kept asking herself.

'Hey, Sidhant, good to see you here,' Avni smiled.

'Hi'

'Hi Sidhant,' Sara said.

Both Avni and Sidhant initiated their evening with drinks. Avni ordered her favorite Margarita and Sidhant asked for a chilled beer. Sara was a teetotaler. She preferred to wait for others before ordering anything. Sidhant was quiet, staring at Sara in between, and Avni was having fun time. Soon rest of the guys arrived and commenced ordering their drinks. Rohit was also a teetotaler, so both Sara and Rohit ordered black coffee. By the time drinks started pouring in for rest of the guys, Avni was too much drunk and she had virtually lost control over herself. She found it difficult to handle herself, so Sara had to request Jimmy to take care of her. Sidhant managed well by keeping a conscious check on himself. It was typical of Sidhant. He got ungovernable, even if he took a little extra, which was followed by vomiting and what not........ It was a regular site in the boy's hostel.

Sara felt uneasy with whatever was happening around, so she was quiet for most of the time, and Sidhant kept staring at her all throughout. God knows, why she never asked him the reason of such a behavior; may be, if she had, it could have saved many lives.

Party was nice. Jimmy dropped Sara and Avni to the hostel. Now, it was time for boy's meet at the hostel. At 'Dawat', it was proposed that it will happen the next day.

Next morning, there was very thin attendance in the class because of hangover. Surprisingly, Avni couldn't make it to the class. Sara, Jimmy and, for a change, Sidhant were there. Jimmy asked about the training report from Sara. Without even looking at him she handed over a file to him.

'Thanks!'

Sara didn't say anything and just moved away from there. Sidhant keenly watched, what was going on. He was a shrewd guy. He recognized, what could have happened.

He smirked, "One more gone ....shot shot...."

He followed Sara to the canteen where she sat alone.

'Can I sit here?'

'Oh sure,' Sara gave him a pleasant smile.

Both of them were quiet and after they finished their tea,

'Let's go', Sara said.

'Yep'

They came back to their lecture room, where they had to face the glances of many people including Avni as they entered the room. Everyone was shocked to see them together. In fact, no one liked it, whether it was Rohit or Jimmy or for no reasons Avni too. They had to sit together in the last row. Even Prof Gupta couldn't digest it, and within few minutes on some ostensible reason asked Sidhant to leave the class. Sidhant gladly moved out as if he was waiting for this to happen. He had no interest in attending the class.

Prof Gupta had been observing Sidhant for the last three years and had a very bad opinion about him. When he saw him with Sara, who was considered to be an ideal student, he couldn't tolerate the thought of Sidhant misleading Sara.

At night in the hostel, boys gathered for their scheduled meeting. Sidhant wasn't there. This time it was a clean hearted discussion, everyone grows with time, so even the boys had grown; although, still the topic of conversation was Avni and her Margarita shots. When everybody dispersed, and only two guys, Rohit and Jimmy were standing, as they were discussing something else and not party, Sidhant arrived. He was completely drunk.

What happened? Did I miss something?

'No, we only enjoyed Avni's state yesterday,' Rohit said.

'She's a nice girl; don't make fun of her,' Sidhant said. Jimmy was astonished to hear it, and for a moment thought, "If anything serious has developed between Sidhant and Avni. I can't afford to lose Avni now. I have already tried my luck with Sara."

'No one talked about Sara,' Sidhant asked.

'There was hardly anything to discuss,' Jimmy said

'I understand, but I don't know why I'm getting obsessed with that arrogant girl.'

I'm cognizant about you guys; you have got your respective share by now, ha ha....', and he fell on the ground, unconscious.

Jimmy and Rohit were zapped for a moment, then picked him up from the floor and took him back to his room.

Next day, Jimmy and Rohit came to Sidhant's room before going to the college.

'Sidhant who told you about Sara and us, even I wasn't aware of anything about Rohit?'

'What?'

'You were saying something when you came here last night'

'You guys know; I was drunk, don't remember iota of what I said.'

'What about Sara?'

'She's too cynical, not my kinds'

'Is it? Jimmy knew he was hiding the truth from them'

Rohit took the initiative and said, 'Sidhant I sense you are madly in love with her; although, I can't say the same about Sara. It's difficult to predict her.'

'Love! ha ha...., last thing on this earth.'

'I have seen my parents, they had a love marriage and since childhood I have been searching for love in their marriage.

'I'm closer to my nanny rather than to my mother.'

'That's inconsolable, but I feel you are getting inclined towards Sara and it's not today, I have been observing you since very first day.

'Not sure if you are afraid of telling her about your feelings or is it your ego, that's stopping you from doing so?'

'Okay see you in the college,' they left the room, and Sidhant stood there, numb!

He got anxious and wanted to fag. Instead of going to college, he straight away went to the canteen, and started smoking there. Without break, for the whole day he sat there, smoking. Everyone in the class was whispering about it, even Sara also heard it, but Jimmy and Rohit knew the reason. They wandered who could be the person to stop him, and ask him to get up from there. Then, they thought about Avni and requested her to help Sidhant.

By then, Sidhant had become a big brother figure for the whole class. Everyone wanted to do something good for him. His character was like that; at times you would like to loath him for what he was, then naturally you would be attracted to his charm of foolish simplicity.

Avni went to him and quietly sat beside him.

'So, have you finished your project report?' Avni said trying to break the lull.

Silence....

'I don't feel you are here to ask me about my project report.'

'Yes.'

'What is it?'

'You seem to be upset.'

'Who told you?'

'I can see you since morning, and moreover, I can get the vibes.'

Sidhant smiled and looked at her, 'Vibes! Are you sure you haven't left Jimmy and have got involved with me.'

Avni laughed,' You bastard....'

'You are fascinating, but still I have my head on my shoulders. You have several great qualities to make any girl run away from you.'

'Oh! Like'

'You are too casual, least bothered about your career, chain smoker....,' she wanted to say drunkard also, but refrained from doing so as she sailed in the same boat.

'Smoking, I can leave it any day if someone asks for it, it depends who asks,' Avni saw him blushing

'Okay, at least, for now, you can leave it for me.'

'Two cup tea, Mohan bhaiya.' They finished their tea; Sidhant walked Avni to the hostel as it was too late in the evening. Sara saw both of them coming. She couldn't understand what was conspiring between them, but she felt jealous for the first time.

In his unconscious state, Sidhant was very right when he labeled Sara, as arrogant. She acted so in certain situations. May be, her super ego forced her to behave so at times. She even didn't ask Avni from where she was coming so late, and if everything was fine with her? She kept quiet, wanting Avni to say something.

Soon after, Avni received a call from Jimmy, so both of them didn't get the time to talk about it.

Third year was about to end. One fine day, Sara sat alone in her class, jotting down some notes. Sidhant also came and sat there. Sara, deliberately, didn't pay any heed to him; although, her heart started beating fast.

After some time, Sidhant said, 'Sara, let's go out for tea.'

'Fine,' as if she was eager to go out with him.

'Let's go to the canteen, near staff club,' Sidhant wanted to be with her, away from the college crowd.

'Why?'

'It's more peaceful and neat.'

'If you want, let's go to our canteen only'

'Okay,' Sidhant knew he had no choice but to agree to her.

They sat there, not saying anything to each other. Suddenly, Sidhant said, 'I think you like me.'

Sara turned nervous, 'How dare you tell me this? What do you think about yourself? Are you Brad Pitt or what?'

'Oh! You are suggesting me that you can't like anyone less than Brad Pitt.'

'Sidhant, you are just trying to manipulate. I never said anything like that. What kind of girl do you consider I am?'

'So, if you like me, you become a bad girl?'

'Stop it here. Fact is, I hate you,' Sara said it in impulse.

It was too immature or arrogant on Sidhant's part to talk to Sara in an offending manner. He could have talked to her softly and expressed his feelings. Instead, he preferred to put her on defense, to know her true feelings. However, in this process he stepped on her ego and made things worse.

Sara would have longed to hear some innocent expression of his love for her.

Sara was coming from a traditional background. She wasn't interested in any short lived relationships. Her pre conceived notions about love was, *"it's something just sensed from the heart. True love is unconditional, and if two people love each other they adjust in any situation. Love can't be based on things which can change any time in life - looks, behavior, attitude, financial status. Compatibility can make you good partners only in static situations and life is not static. Love is something eternal."*

Sidhant took Sara's response in a very negative way, "If she loves me, she will be demeaned because she never considers me capable of anything." This was his complex or bias for Sara which made him think so. She would have died to hear, "I love you," from him.

Sidhant's ego flared up; he left the place in hurry leaving Sara alone, saying, *'Fine, my doors would be always open for you; you can enter them anytime in your life.'*

Sara didn't take this part 'in life' seriously. She thought, "He is being melodramatic."

Sara was always apprehensive about him, "What if he is trying to play with my emotions or trying to prove his heroism in front of others." It was also his protean attitude which made Sara skeptical about him.

She wanted to rush back home immediately, but it was Wednesday; two days left for weekend. She was too depressed and that was visible on her face.

Ultimately, she went back that weekend, and as soon as she reached home her mother told her that Diya had cleared 'IIT'. Sara was overwhelmed, and decided to go with the flow. Everyone was calling to congratulate Diya. Sara was very happy for her younger sister.

On Monday morning, she went to the hostel with a box of sweets, and shared it with everyone in the hostel; took it to the college as well. Initially, everybody got an impression that she was engaged; only to know later that her younger sister had cracked IIT.

That year everyone was going into different companies for summer training. Sixth semester exams got finished and class dispersed for their homes and further for trainings.

Restlessness had now become part of Sara's life. She was confused, so much so, that she couldn't even concentrate on her training. This time she did it for the heck of it. It was strange, this time she wanted to go back to the college as early as possible, to see Sidhant. She was feeling guilty if in any way she had hurt him.

College resumed in first week of August, everyone was excited to meet each other and on top of it, they were in their last year.

Sara was eager to have a glimpse of Sidhant, and finally, he arrived on the first day but totally ignored her.

Life continued....

Whenever, Sidhant got a chance he kept gazing at Sara; even one day for an hour or so. After such experiences Sara used to perceive, "Whatever I have done is absolutely right. He's just making fun of me by creating scenes and if my family, finds me going around with such a boy they would be shattered. It can even impact Diya's future."

But her heart ached, and she desperately wanted someone to assure her that he was sincere and loved her. On one hand she discerned, "love is immutable", and on the other hand she always wanted reassurance about Sidhant. She was afraid of accepting it. Fear of being deceived by him always haunted her. Sidhant was so right, when he said that she was too confused.

One day, they had a practical in 'Machine design lab', which was not within the college but just a few miles away. These were common labs for campus school students of senior classes and engineering folks. When everyone was entering into machine design lab; Sidhant, suddenly opened the door of physics lab and started looking for someone. Then, he waived his hand and closed the door.

Rohit and Sara were walking together. Sara, out of curiosity asked Rohit, 'What was he doing?' Rohit hesitantly said, 'Prof Gupta's daughter is in campus school'

'So, what has that got to do with Sidhant?'

'He's flirting with her and she is inside'

'Oh shit! What a man he is?'

'Only God knows!'

The reason, Sara, could never make up her mind about him was his this awful behavior; totally unpredictable. Look at the extent; it was Prof Gupta's daughter this time. He knew about it and that's why he was always so biased about Sidhant. No one was sure why he was doing it; to make Sara jealous or was he just having fun?

Sara's intuition immediately told her, "He is trying to make me jealous."

Was this Sara's love for Sidhant that she shielded any act of his, or was she being foolish or clumsy? These were the questions which anybody would deliberate about, when framing an opinion about her. But in reality, she was also not clear about herself. As the time was passing by, she was getting more and more caught in a trap. Sara being an introvert creature never tried discussing it with anyone, not even with her mother or sister. There was an internal fight going on within her and she felt, as if, she was losing the battle of life.

No one could have imagined, but it was Avni who came to her rescue. Once, while they were coming back from the college, Avni initiated an intimate and candid conversation with Sara.

'Sara, you might find it absurd or may even consider it as an intrusion into your privacy, but I can tell you that there's something heavy on your mind. If you consider me worthwhile, you can share it with me'

Sara was calm and didn't react in any either ways.

After sometime, she said, 'Avni, I know we are friends and also two different personalities. But it's a fact your personality has never kept me away from you. Since childhood, I have found it difficult to get too much close to anyone. I appreciate your concern for me and your judgment about me.'

There are moments in everyone's life when you can't hold more than a limit, and it becomes essential to vent out. It was that day for Sara.

'You know, Sidhant told me that I like him.

'In these four years, we have hardly spoken to each other and as per my memory; I have never given him any impression, of me, liking him in any ways. He has been always misbehaving with me, projecting himself like a Romeo. It is too shameless on his part to tell me such a thing.

'I'm totally confused about him.'

Avni was not at all shocked and simply asked, 'Do you like him?'

'I don't find there's any reason to like him.'

'Do you perceive, liking comes with reasons or simply you like a person?'

Avni was trying to help Sara to explore her heart, but Sara Sara............ something was stopping her from speaking the truth. After recent incident, it was all the more difficult for her to introspect honestly.

'Of course, even if you simply like a person how can you verify that there aren't some unrealized reasons behind it!' Sara said.

'Don't make it a GD (Group discussion), try to answer me in yes or no, whether you like him or not?'

'No'

'Then things are clear, and why are you getting so upset about it? He approached you for whatever reasons, it's his whim. You said 'No', that's your wish. I don't understand where the problem is?'

'The problem is, the way he is trying to put it on me.'

'Okay! If he would have proposed you, are you fine with it?'

'No, I never said that.'

'Sara, you are such a brilliant student; why are you wasting your time on what Sidhant has done, better focus on your preparations. It's high time!

Sara knew, still she hasn't confided her truth in Avni and again hoping for reassurance said, 'I'm feeling guilty, if in anyways I have hurt his feelings and in case he is sincere.'

'And if he is?'

'Something can be thought about it positively,' Sara said.

'Avni, you tell me frankly, what do you know about him?' Sara knew, "Avni must have been getting some feedback about it from Jimmy. Boys are usually not as secretive as girls are in expressing their emotions, so Sidhant must have told something to Jimmy."

'Look Sara, Sidhant is crazy about you and I can't say whether its infatuation or anything long lived. Being mindful of him, I can tell you, it can be a temporary obsession which will die down when you enter into a relationship.'

This came as a blow to Sara. Something she was afraid of even accepting within herself, has been said by Avni.

'It's your life; you are free to do anything but my personal advice to you is forget him and focus on your preparations'

'True, it's a great help,' Sara said.

Sidhant was on her mind every time, but she couldn't explain the reason for it even to herself. She tried listening to Avni, and started focusing on her MBA preparations. But every time she got a chance she tried being nice to Sidhant; however, he completely avoided her.

Sara, inwardly, called it end of the story or there was never any story.

She became busy in her tutorials. College, tutorials and then college; life started moving in circles. She became completely involved in herself and Sidhant was only a vague memory or she considered so.

CHAPTER 5

*M*BA ENTRANCE EXAMS STARTED; and they used to be normally on weekends. Sara was going home every Friday evening for it. It was becoming too hectic for her, but then, she was a girl with strong will power who wanted to make a mark in life. She chose to appear for five entrance exams. Like every other MBA aspirant, IIM was her first priority. Four other colleges came in her second priority list.

It was first week of December; Sara had her CAT exam on Sunday. She appeared for a mock test one day before it, and then, as her usual self, decided to have few relaxing hours before exam; she had prepared well, and she was sure, her strong background would add on to it.

Sara left home for the exam at around 8:30 a.m. Exam was to start at 10:00 a.m. She anticipated traffic to be much less in comparison to a normal weekday.

"It should be a one hour drive till examination centre on weekend," she thought. Human beings can only think and desire, but ultimately no one knows what our destiny has in stored for us. She insisted to drive on her own to the center, but like any other typical Indian father, Sara's father rebuffed her idea by saying that it was a critical exam; and with this kind of stress on her mind, it's not safe for her to drive in such a chaotic traffic. He decided to accompany Sara, not letting her drive.

Look at the irony; when she was one mile away from the center, an auto rickshaw smashed into their car and the auto toggled. It was a miraculous escape for the auto driver; although, his life was saved but he got some serious injuries on his legs, face and his one arm was, seemingly broken. Immediately, they were surrounded by a huge crowd and in such cases, irrespective of who's at fault, mob sympathy goes with the weaker party. Mob started being rude to Sara's father. Sara panicked. Her father advised her to take some vehicle and go from there. She refused to do so as crowd was getting rowdy; they were talking of calling police, so in such a situation Sara refused to leave her father and go.

Then he literally shouted at her, 'Sara go from here. You are already late. We are not at fault, so nothing will happen to me. I'll take care of everything, you leave immediately.' Sara not knowing, what to do commenced her march towards the venue. On seeing her running like this in trepidation, a passerby stopped, and after listening to her, offered to drop her to the examination center. She was there in next five minutes, but she was late for the exam by ten minutes. Anybody would know, ten minutes delay for CAT exam could be catastrophic, and that too, in such a timorous state would have meant battle already lost. Sara still tried giving it a fight, and was there till the last moment. She wasn't too happy about her performance, yet for her, it wasn't all gone. She took a cab and came back home. She didn't find her father back from that catastrophe. He came in the late evening, very worried about Sara. Finding Sara composed he was relieved, but for days to come he felt penitence on his decision; and he commiserated his daughter.

Monday morning, Sara reached back to her college, a bit relaxed; at least, a big hurdle was out of her way. She was not thinking about the outcome at the moment. But she was also not pessimistic either. When she reached the college, her batch mates were discussing about New Year celebrations. This lightened her mood, and she tried involving herself in the preparations. Sidhant resurfaced on her mind or we can assume he insured that he never disappeared from there. His eyes were always haunting her and she never knew what to do. She had no idea how to break this deadlock of wide open eyes and tightly sealed lips. She just ignored....

New Year party was organized in the college auditorium. Everyone was ecstatic about that year as it could have proved to be a turning point in their lives. Hardly anyone was in their senses that day, it was wine everywhere. Sara, Rohit and a few others, were not having liquor that day, rest everyone was drunk. King of wine, Sidhant, decided to surprise everyone by being a teetotaler on the occasion. He was sitting quietly in a corner doing nothing, but his favorite pass time. Sara was embarrassed; she wanted to slap him for his behavior, but like every other time she preferred to be oblivious of it.

Sara and Avni got a special permission to stay out till midnight; so, as the clock struck 12 o'clock they had to rush back to their hostels. Sara hardly slept for few hours then she left for her home. She wanted to be with her family on New Year.

※　　※　　※

Back home; Diya received an invitation from her friend for high tea, at his residence. She asked Sara to accompany her. Sara was too tired so she wanted to say 'no' to her little sister. But her mother insisted her to go, as Diya might get late while coming back and she wanted Sara to escort her.

Sara, in her final year, has learnt to spruce up, and had started giving attention to looks. Sara and Diya dressed up nicely; they were looking chics. Sara drove Diya to her friend Ankit's house. Sara bought a box of dry fruits on their way for gift. It took them hardly thirty minutes to reach his residence. It was a nice, cozy house, in the posh area of Greater Kailash. Ankit was a charming guy. He took them inside, to his parents. It was a pleasant, sophisticated and educated family. Sara was happy to meet them.

After sometime, other guests started trickling in. Gathering comprised mainly of Ankit's college mates and a few of close family friends and relatives.

'Hi; Sara, there's someone who wants to meet you,' Sara turned her face and saw, a young Richard Gere standing along with Ankit, feeling a bit embarrassed.

'Nope, I just asked who she is, as I have never seen her in the college,' Medhansh said.

'So, you don't want to meet her; it's okay........'

'No! No! I don't mean that.'

Sara blushed and said, ' What is it Ankit?'

'Jokes apart; I want you to meet Medhansh, a final year student of our college and a good friend of mine.

'He must be your batch mate; you guys might be interested in discussing future, Oh sorry! Your career plans,' Ankit smirked.

'Hi; I'm Sara, final year REC............'

'I'm Medhansh, Nice meeting you,' and they started talking.

It was 8:00 p.m.; Sara asked Diya to call it a day. They bid good- bye to everyone, and pushed back to their home. Sara was very tired, as she had travelled in the morning and attended late night party a day before, so she fell asleep as soon as they reached back. She never recalled Medhansh after that day. It was just a passed by meeting for her. She stayed at home for one more day and then went back.

There, at the college, it was time for campus placements and also end of the semester. Sara was determined to go for MBA, so she decided not to appear for campus placements. However, she heard, Sidhant was trying for the same Bangalore based Company, where he did his second year training. Sara thought, "It will be good if he gets through; otherwise what he'll do." But then, it was none of her business.

Avni and Jimmy decided to pursue Master's in the same college.

Sara went back for her last entrance exam of 'Faculty of Management Studies' (FMS). It went well, and she was optimistic about her performance. While she was moving out of the entrance exam, she saw Medhansh,

'What a coincidence? Hi', Sara said.

'Hello; how was your exam?'

'I'm hopeful'

'What about you?'

'It was fine. Anyways, I'm not keen to pursue any further studies. I have already got through an IT MNC and they are paying me well too'

'That's good! See you again Medhansh, keep well,' Sara said walking hurriedly towards her car. While driving, Sara realized that Medhansh wanted to say her something but she didn't give him any chance. When she reached back home she mentioned about Medhansh to Diya and also what she felt. Diya asked her to take it easy and ignore it. Sara was okay with it as he was Diya's senior and if she wasn't concerned, so was Sara.

Sara went back and got involved with her semester exams. It went well and she could maintain her top position.

Meanwhile, results for CAT were out. She couldn't get through IIM, as anybody could have anticipated. But as Sara was sanguine, so she got temporarily depressed.

A few days later, Sara received a pleasant surprise. She got a call from her mother in late hours of the evening on one of those days. She came to know that she had cleared 'FMS' written Exam, to be followed with a Group Discussion and Interview.

It weighed heavily on her mind and she was restless the entire night.

As the morning set in, she had resolved to take the demon of Group Discussion and Interview head on.

Entire next week, she browsed through all the relevant literature she found in her college Library. Life got confined in a room for Sara.

Saturday, was the day of her test: her grit, patience, knowledge, perhaps everything. She reached home by Friday evening and by next day noon, she was through with everything.

After a month, Sara's dad rushed in home with box of sweets in hands and joy written on his face. He just hugged Sara. She stood there speechless .She couldn't believe her destiny for a while, but she understood the news was good for her.

Her efforts had been rewarded; she got admission to one of the most Premier Management Institutes of India. It was a matter of big solace for her. She had got a right direction in her career. No one knows what lies in future ahead. How priorities would change in life? But for now, getting admission to MBA was her top most priority and she was thrilled. She wanted to spend rest of her time in college in a joyful manner- no fights or controversies with anyone.

It was the last semester and everyone could see a change in Sara's attitude. She was a calm lot. She had started mingling with her batch mates and was far friendlier. She wanted to part off at a very good note with everyone. Sara always believed in goodness of human beings and considered bad part to be situational. She desired to keep good memories of people.

On a wintery day in the afternoon, it was 'Advanced Robotics' class. It was sunny, so guys decided to bunk the class and play a cricket match, instead. Jimmy called up Avni and gave her the message. As usual, Avni was fine with it, but she got involved in gossiping with other girls and couldn't convey the message to Sara. Sara was waiting for Avni to go along with her to the class. When she didn't turn up for long, Sara decided to proceed alone towards the college. Sara was relaxed but not non serious. She reached the classroom and found it empty. She realized there was something which she was unaware of, so she started moving out of the room but at the same time Prof Tripathi, Advanced Robotics, teacher came in. He asked Sara, 'Where are you going?'

'Sir, no one has come; I feel they have planned a mass bunk'

Prof Tripathi got furious and said, 'So what? I'm going to take my class even if it's one student.

'Already everyone in your class is falling short of attendance including you, Sara, and hardly two lectures are left.'

Sara knew, "If I attend the lecture today whole class would be failed on the pretext of shortfall of attendance as Professor is exasperated this time. And if, I also don't attend it, there is a fair chance of rescheduling of the class." Sara decided to say 'no' to the professor in larger interests.

'Sorry sir, I won't be able to attend the class when everyone's future is at stake.'

'No problem, Sara; I'll see to it that no one is able to appear in this subject.'

Sara came back very upset. Avni was looking for her desperately. Seeing her entering the hostel she immediately rushed towards her and said, 'Sorry, I'm late. Jimmy called up to inform, "There won't be any Robotics class today."'

Sara yelled at Avni, 'So you knew it. How could you not tell me that on priority? Now face it! Everyone shall get F, Prof Tripathi has threatened me.'

Avni rushed towards the phone and called up Jimmy,' Jimmy, Jimmy, told everything to him....'

'Don't worry its everyday drama; he won't do anything. Say thanks to Sara for the stand she took.'

For the days to come, it was a big issue in the college. Prof Tripathi refused to take even remaining two classes, as he said it was of no use because everyone was short of attendance and he won't conduct the exam. He became so rigid that he even refused to listen to the college Dean.

Sara went crazy. It meant delaying the degree by few more months and she won't get admission anywhere that year. . Her world was ruined. She fell sick and came back home. Diya shared it with her friends, and news also reached to Medhansh.

Medhansh along with Ankit came rushing in to see Sara. Medhansh was shocked to find her in that state. She became numb; she lost her complete appetite and was looking so fragile.

For no rhyme or reason, Medhansh went to famous 'Hanuman temple,' walked barefooted for 20 miles. He prayed for Sara's speedy recovery and brought some prasad for her. He pleaded Sara to have it. Sara became emotional and went into tears.' Medhansh! I shall lose my admission this year, student of the batch title everything...,'

'Everything would be okay Sara, and why are you so upset because of these petty materialistic things? Life is so long, you can always get them anytime. Who cares about that title! You are already student of the batch as you have sacrificed so much for them.'

Sara felt invigorated, and was listening to Medhansh patiently. He gave her some juice.

Although after two or three days she was still woebegone, but she had started partially recovering.

Her classmates came to know about her condition, and now and then someone was calling to enquire about her well being.

Avni was in constant touch with her. Sidhant never called up and in that frame of mind too, Sara was expecting a call from him.

Final exams were about to start so she decided to go back. Looking at her state, her mother also accompanied her till the time she was perfectly okay.

As soon as she reached the college, Avni told her that Prof Tripathi had agreed to take some classes to compensate for attendance shortfall and after observing the seriousness of students he might also conduct the exam.

Now you could attribute it to the magic of Medhansh prayers or if logically analyzed, this was bound to happen. No one is that cruel to play with the future of so many students. Professor wanted to teach them a lesson; after all they had been harassing him for so long. It was his turn then.

Anyways, everything is well that ends well.

At home, Sara's parents were really wondering why Medhansh would take such hardships for Sara as they hardly knew each other. Even Diya and Ankit were also amazed at his emotional heroic gesture. Diya had an idea about Medhansh colorful past so she never took him that seriously.

⁓❧   ⁓❧   ⁓❧

Sara was so excited that she thought of calling Medhansh.

'Hi Medhansh, this is Sara.'

'Great to hear your chirpy voice; Diya informed me, everything is settled at your end.'

'Yep and in fact, I have called you to say thanks. Without hurting your feelings, I must confess that I never have credence on such superstitious things, yet your action gave me a lot of strength.'

'Even I'm also not illusory, but don't know what happened that I couldn't control myself.'

'Anyways, thanks a ton for whatever you did.'

'Anything for you Sara,' Sara hung up the phone. She definitely didn't understand the meaning of his last sentence but preferred to brush it off.

Exams started and theory was completed within ten days. Practical and the project presentation were remaining. One of those days after practical, Sara invited everyone for tea. All except Sidhant joined her at the canteen. Sidhant was stuck somewhere in his practical and was still not out of the lab. Sara requested Rohit to wait for him and invite him once he was done. It was more than an hour. Everyone took their tea and went away, but still she couldn't see Rohit and Sidhant. She almost assumed that they were not coming, than in between trees she saw two heads emerging and moving towards her. Sara ordered three cups of tea and sat with them. Hardly anybody talked to each other. Jimmy came forward to break the ice and started some irrelevant discussion.

Sara asked, 'Sidhant how was your practical.'

Without even looking at her, he said, 'Okay.'

Jimmy realized, "both of them talking amicably to each other is an uphill task." So he decided to leave the place and allow them to struggle with their prejudices and larger than life ego's. He made an excuse and moved away from there.

It was cloudy, greenery all around; birds were chirping, suggesting them to make a new beginning. Two of them were still quiet, not even looking at each other; however, in between Sara looked at him so as to tell him to say something. He was silent, disinterested. Sara thought he might be depressed because he hadn't been able to crack any MBA entrance and again she had out passed him so he might be feeling hesitant in talking to her.

Sara said, 'How was your stay in the college?'

'Good, nothing extraordinary; excuse me,' Sidhant went away and Sara was sitting alone in the canteen. Nothing could have been more humiliating for Sara than this. She found it so rude and considered she was right in holding a biased opinion about him. He didn't have etiquettes to handle a girl......she felt everything negative whatever she could think about him. She started marching towards her hostel completely lost in her thoughts, "It is wrong on my part trying to part off on a healthy note with everyone. You shouldn't care about some people at all, and Sidhant is one of those creatures. Enough is enough. Now I'm not going to appease him anymore. There's no guilt on my mind. I'm done with him."

In another one week, all practical and presentations were over. The class said good- bye to the college and moved ahead to explore what future has comprised for them.

She was happy to be at home, but there was an uneasiness which followed her and she started taking it in a stride. How so ever upset she was with Sidhant but his thoughts warmed the cockles of Sara's heart and she could never explore the rationale behind it.

It was time to commemorate at home. After four years their daughter had come back, of course, to go again, but for now they wanted to enjoy her achievement. Diya planned a party at home. Ankit was helping her in all the spadework. She invited first family and few friends for the occasion. Friends included some of the Sara's school classmates, neighborhood friends and a few of Diya's friends. Medhansh was also an invitee as he was now a common friend.

It was a nice simple evening. Sara was very fond of wearing whites so she chose to wear a white top and denim jeans that day. She was tall, delicate but a curvy girl, and being fair skinned every color looked well on her. She was looking sober yet fetching.

Guests started pouring in at around 5:00 o'clock. Sara was meeting her schoolmates after four years. One of her friend, Shalini, who used to be plumpy nerd, was now looking like a cool chic. Sara took some time to recognize her, and was flabbergasted to see her in new Avtaar. Shalini was a brilliant medical student and she was doing her MBBS from 'AIIMS'. She was a scholar but that day she appeared like a supermodel. Another fast friend of her whom she met in XII standard, Namrita, also made it to the party. She used to be a simple, loving and caring girl and was still looking like the same old self.

Overwhelmed to see old pals, Sara wanted this time to go on till the face in the blue. Medhansh also appeared along with Ankit but Sara couldn't focus much on him.

Sara told Ankit and Medhansh, 'Sorry guys, we are a teetotaler family; can't serve you drinks.'

'I accept your apologies, but don't feel sorry for Medhansh, he is himself a teetotaler. I'm a typical Punjabi, there's no party for me without non veg and drinks.'

'I owe you a dinner, we can plan it anytime next week,' Sara said to Ankit.

'Invite me also; I don't take non veg or drink, doesn't mean I'll not die to have your company,' Medhansh remarked.

Silence..........

'I mean to have all of yours company.....' he tried to cover him up but it was quite evident what he wanted to say.

'Sure, you are equally important to us.'

It was late night; everyone has left for their homes. What a memorable day for Sara? That evening was a reminiscent of her beautiful school days. Sara was feeling rejuvenated, but she was tired too. Diya and Sara decided to call it a day. They went to their rooms and Sara was asleep as soon as she fell on the bed.

One day Diya came back from the college in the evening and said, 'Sara, have you promised a dinner to Ankit, he is remembering it.'

'Yep, let's fix it on this Friday.'

'Do invite Medhansh also on my behalf.'

'Why Medhansh?'

'He wanted to be a part of it; why are you staring at me? He asked for the invite.'

'Shameless, anyways I'll tell him,' Diya said. Diya was sure; Sara won't fall for a guy like Medhansh. But she always maintained a distance with Sara as she was her elder sister, and never asked anything beyond limits.

Diya, passed on the message to both Ankit and Medhansh, and a dinner was confirmed for Friday.

On Friday, Diya called up in the evening, 'Sara, Ankit and I won't be able to make it for the dinner as two hours extra class has been scheduled.'

'No issues, let's plan it for some other day; inform Medhansh also about it,' Sara remarked.

'No, No; I'm in a hurry to rush back to the class, you call up Medhansh.'

'Fine'

'Okay, bye.'

Sara called up Medhansh and told him about the whole situation. She felt apologetic and asked him to make it convenient on some other day. However, for Medhansh this opportunity came as a boon and he would have done anything to meet Sara alone, over a dinner.

'Sara, if you don't mind, can we go? You are free and I'm also in that frame of mind. Let's have some nice time together,' Medhansh said cajoling Sara.

Sara was not too comfortable with these cheesy talks of boys; she always found them acting over smart. She had observed

Medhansh indulging in such talks more than often in the recent past so she had a reason to avoid him.

'Medhansh, I'm still not earning. I can't afford two treats,' she said teasingly. It was a clumsy excuse, but Sara couldn't think of something better at that time.

'You don't worry; it's on me this time. You just gimme your precious time,' cheesy again..........

'No, it's not the question of precious time. I need to ask my parents. I don't know how they would react to my going alone with you,' it was Sara's another excuse as she really wanted to avoid him.

'Don't worry I'll call uncle and seek his permission,' Sara didn't want to make it so formal and create suspicions in his father's mind.

'Please, it's not required; I'll handle it at my end'

'So, we are meeting today at the same place'

'Okay'

CHAPTER 6

SARA WAS PHLEGMATIC ABOUT this meeting; however, she had a slight negative bias. She dressed up casually, picked up her dad's car and reached the venue right on time. She was happy to find Medhansh already waiting there for her. It's little embarrassing for a girl, especially for a pretty girl to sit alone in a restaurant and wait for someone. Every passer by male gives you a gaze, as if he wants to give you the company; but the only problem is the lady walking along with him. And if he's alone, and descent too, then he's afraid of girl's reaction in public.

'Hi Sara, good to see you,'

'Hi, how are you?'

'Feeling great after seeing you,' cheesy again.....

Sara giggled....

'Let's go inside,' Medhansh pushed the door of the restaurant for Sara. He could have waited for the guard sitting there to open it but somehow he was being too courteous. They occupied a table reserved for them. There was silence for a minute. Both of them were moving their heads as if trying to avoid eye contact then suddenly Medhansh said, 'What would you like to drink?'

'Black coffee.'

'Can you have dinner after coffee?'

'It's not a problem.'

'Waiter....'

'One black coffee for the lady and gimme one Coke'

'You want to keep things simple; you are resistant to make changes and you are moody.'

'What do you mean?'

'Your choice of coffee reflects your personality and black coffee takers are usually simple ...'

'You are right to an extent, but your point on resistant to make changes doesn't go too well with my personality. I'm ready to make changes if I'm convinced but yes on certain points I belong to old school of thought,' Sara told with conviction.

'Like!' Medhansh was inquisitive. Sara was going with the flow.......

'Love; I consider, true love happens only once in a lifetime. I really don't understand when people love someone and marry someone else. Either they never loved anyone at first place or they befool themselves by saying that we have moved on.'

'Oh! That's dangerous!' Medhansh's curiosity was now changing into his anxiety

'Why do you say so?' Medhansh wanted to utilize his knowledge about personalities and wanted to play this gamble. Sara seemed to be straight forward and ardent lover of honesty.

'You know I was deeply in love with a girl who studied in girl's college adjacent to our campus. Her name was Meghna. I knew her for more than two years and it was only last year that she got married. Oh! I'm sorry, she was forced to marry. I'm sure she would have given her life before even thinking about leaving me, but then at times you have to yield in front of the circumstances.

'Oh! I'm boring you with my lugubrious past. Let's discuss about your future plans,' Medhansh said with his fingers crossed, awaiting Sara's interest in his life history.

'No please continue, you'll feel good,' Sara being an innocent person tried to prompt him to say something which he was eager to utter.

'Okay, if you insist. My uncle's daughter kamna studied in that college and I used to visit her or she called me whenever we had to go back to our homes. One day when I visited her, she was standing with a very beautiful catty eyed girl. At that time I was really shy of girls and didn't feel comfortable talking to them. So I ignored her and straight away looked into my cousin's eyes.

'She was so vivacious; she immediately said, "Kamna, Will you not like to introduce him?"

'"Sure, he's my cousin Medhansh, studying in nearby engineering college, IIT," Kamna said looking at her.......,' Pause...., meanwhile Medhansh got lost somewhere.

'Meghna!' Sara said to bring him back on the track.

'Oh no, she was Neerja,' Medhansh continued.

'I was blushing like girls but she was bold and seemed to be in a mood to rag me. "Although, you engineering college guys are an intelligent lot, but you are unfortunate in one aspect-you hardly get to see girls and that too beautiful like me in your college. What's your ultimate aim in life- to make a good career? Why do you do that? Because you want best girl to marry you and when I say best, I mean for most of you, a beautiful girl to marry you. When you don't find them in your own colleges, you become a desperate lot and your life goes into limbo. Then colleges like ours come to your rescue. We offer you a combination of beauty and brain. I know, you don't need brain but consider this as an add on."

'She wasn't ready to stop anywhere, and I was getting embarrassed in front of Kamna. I was a simple guy, but not an idiot, to listen so much from a stranger. I kept quiet due to kamna and then interrupted her by saying that we would meet some other time, I had to leave for some important work at college.

'"Nice meeting you!" Neerja said.

'"Same here," and I rushed back towards the college without even doing the work for which I had gone to Kamna.

'After few days, I got a message in the hostel I had some visitors. I came out to see who it was, that early in the morning, around 7:00 am. I was shocked to see Neerja and Kamna standing there. I could see, intentionally they had come early to avoid stares of the guys. That is the time usually boys are asleep. I was red with anger and whispered to Kamna, "You could have called me, why have you come here?"

'Neerja immediately realized what was transpiring between us. She said, "It's me, who has forced her to come here. It's my birthday today, and I want to invite you for a small get together in the evening at 'Dragon' restaurant."

'"Wish you a very Happy Birthday!"

'"Thanks, hope you'll come. There's no need to get a gift, but in case you want to bring something then Perfume can be the best option. I like wearing Elizabeth Arden," Neerja said.

'I wondered, "How straightforward she is!" But there was something in her that appealed me and I looked forward to meet her at the 'Dragon'.

'In the evening, I was there with a perfume in my hand, nicely gift wrapped. I once again wished her happy birthday and got seated with Kamna. Neerja was busy welcoming her guests and collecting gifts. After few minutes Neerja marched towards us with a drink in her hand. She offered me the drink and I refused by saying, "I don't drink." It was visible from her face that she was offended. I didn't understand the reason. She got soft drinks for us and we started chatting. She shared with me that she was a bollywood freak and she was also fond of music, that too 'gazals'. I smiled as we shared the common interests. We further started discussing about singers and I realized her favorite gazal's singer was 'Jagjit Singh', which was mine too. If someone listens this, he or she would definitely feel that I was trying to flirt with her. Candidly, there was nothing on my mind.'

Sara interrupted him in between, 'If you are saying it to know my opinion, please be rest assured I'm only listening to you and not analyzing what you are telling.' Medhansh smiled and continued.........

'We had a rare old time that evening**.** I escorted both of them to the hostel and when I bid them good- bye, Neerja scoffingly suggested me to come in. I said, "Some other day as it's too late." Then, dragging the conversation, she suggested me to stay there and leave the next day. She said I seemed to be smart enough to make my way inside the hostel. Anyways, I evaded a reply and said them good-bye.

This way, we started meeting quite often, sometimes with Kamna and at times, without her. I felt as if I have started liking her. Her authority and possessiveness made me feel owned, and I was enjoying it. One day, she suggested me to go on an outdoor trip for 2-3 days. I asked her, how she would manage her college and hostel. She said she would give a medical certificate and tell hostel warden that she was moving to her local guardians for a day or two. I could also have easily managed it but don't know why, preferred to defer it by taking work as an excuse. In fact, I wasn't clear about my feelings for Neerja. Moreover, I was also short of funds that month, and in our country girls expect boys to pay for everything when they are going out with them, "joking ...ha ha." But that incident gave me a feeling that she was getting fascinated by me, and wanted to take our relationship to the next level. I knew I wasn't prepared for it yet.'

'Let's order some dinner first otherwise you'll get late', Medhansh suggested to Sara.

'Yep, I'll have Mushroom Barley soup and white pasta. What about you?'

'I'm fond of typical Indian food; bread and yellow dal'

'Soup'

'Yes I'll have Cream of tomato.' Medhansh ordered the dinner and came back to his story.

'I got busy with my studies as semester exams were nearing, so for the next one month I didn't visit kamna or Neerja nor they called me up.

'After finishing my exams and before leaving for home, I thought of meeting Kamna; to be honest, Neerja. I called for both of them when I went to the hostel. Kamna wasn't there as she had gone shopping with some other friends. My uncle is an affluent man and Kamna is their only daughter, so shopping is her pass time. I knew she's not going to come before late evening. Meanwhile, Neerja appeared along with a wheatish, short statured girl; who wasn't attractive at all, at the first look. Both of them were looking total contrasts.

"'Hi Medhansh, after a long time!"

"'Yes, I was busy with my exams, finished the last one today itself."

"'How nice, and within minutes you are here at the girl's hostel.' I felt it too embarrassing in front of a stranger. Neerja could make it out, and quickly changed the track .Then she introduced me to the girl with her,

"'She's Meghna, fresher in our college."

"'Hi," and as soon as I heard that she's a fresher; I got sympathetic towards her, and to make her feel comfortable said, "Hope you are having a good time and no one is harassing you here. Anyways, this ragging is only for initial few days but the friends you make during this process go a long way."

'Before Meghna could say anything, Neerja interrupted and said, "You are lucky to find such a wise preacher so early, and in case you aren't comfortable here, he can take you to his hostel."

'This time, I couldn't resist myself and told Neerja, "It is getting too sarcastic."

'I could see on her face that she was hurt but so were we, Meghna and I.

'"Don't worry! She's with me and nobody can dare to say her anything! Now she's not a fresher, she's Neerja ma'am's friend. I have shifted her to my room, and till the time she's comfortable with the hostel environment she can stay with me," Neerja said smilingly.

'This aspect of her personality really made her adorable. She was always eager to extend her support to the needy. All this while, I and Neerja were chatting, Meghna didn't even utter a word. She even didn't say me hello. I told them that I was leaving for home and would be back in two days, and then we could plan to meet again. When I was leaving the place, I heard a polite voice saying "bye"; it was Meghna.

'When I came back from home, I thought of going to Kamna's hostel as my mother had sent some goodies for her. But we friends decided to go for a movie and I changed my program. Next morning, when I was passing by the visitor's room, I saw Neerja sitting with Ravi. Ravi was the most notorious guy of our campus, a typical Richie rich. For a moment, I didn't believe my eyes and then I re looked at her to confirm that she was Neerja. A guy standing outside the room told me that she was Ravi's cousin. Anyways, I didn't say anything and came back quietly to my room, hoping, who so ever he might be, she would definitely meet me before leaving. The whole day had gone by, but no one called me and I just spent the day lying on my bed. I got up in the evening and straight away went to the visitor's room to see if still she was there. There was no one. I was disappointed and kept wondering why didn't she meet me before leaving? I felt humiliated and thought of retaliating.

Next day, I went to Kamna's hostel, only asked for her and not Neerja. Kamna came out, but that day she was with Meghna. I said hello to Meghna and handed over the stuff to Kamna. To my surprise, I saw Meghna staring at me in between. I left the place and came back to hostel. After a few days I got a call from Neerja, and she invited me for a get together. I said I would come and once again I went there on the scheduled date and time. It was a very small gathering of very close friends- Kamna, Meghna and to my shock Ravi also dropped in. Neerja was aware that Ravi and I were from the same college so she introduced us in a very quintessential way, "I know, you must be knowing each other; turning her face towards Ravi she said, "Medhansh is Kamna's cousin." I could clearly see from Ravi's face that he gave a damn to, who I were, he immediately wanted to turn me out of that place. It was the most formal get together I had attended in the past few years. An aura of stress and uneasiness was there everywhere in the environment. Only Meghna was away from all this; she kept looking at me in between and was showering her smiles now and then. She wanted to talk to me but refrained to do so in public. Party ended and it was a big relief to move out of that place. I felt sick beyond anyone's imagination.

'Kamna and I were going to attend a marriage in family. We decided to go together on a train. I picked up Kamna from her hostel and we reached the railway station. No sooner we got into the train we started chatting. Of course, our common topic nowadays was Neerja, and to add on to it, it was Meghna also. As it was already bothering my mind, first thing I asked Kamna was Neerja's relationship with Ravi. Kamna told me that he was Neerja's boy friend, and this time Neerja was genuinely serious, as Ravi was a rich man's son studying in a reputed college and she couldn't have desired for anything more than that. I got astonished to listen it. I had not shared with Kamna about Neerja proposing me an outstation trip just one month back. I preferred to keep quiet. After Neerja, we started discussing about Meghna and Kamna had a wicked smile on her face. When I asked her the reason, she counter questioned me on my visit to her hostel when I met Meghna for the first time. I told her that yes I met them as she had gone out for shopping. Meghna seemed quite afraid and she even didn't utter a single word during my whole conversation with Neerja. Kamna intervened, "Precisely, I know what happened that day. Neerja like usual crossed her limits. You handled her patiently but firmly, and that has made Meghna crazy about you.'

'"Meghna and me"

'"So what, She's a very nice and loving girl. Her father is such a high profile man yet she is so humble."

'"I'm still not convinced; please don't share our discussions with Meghna."

'We reached home; family marriages are real fun. Good food, dance and frolic everywhere. Each one is so excited; they want to be part of every ritual. Kamna and I had a good time, and we made it a point not to discuss about Neerja or Meghna after that.

'While we were coming back, I said, "Kamna, one of these days I would visit your hostel."

'She replied, "Meghna will be very happy to see you."

'Whether you believe it or not, knowing that someone is giving you attention makes you anxious. I wanted to know more about Meghna.

'When I reached back, I met Ravi in the hostel corridor. He stopped me, "I want to tell you something, keep away from Neerja. Even if she tries to get in touch with you, avoid her."

'I got furious. I told him, "It's my life and you should better keep away from it."

'Ravi threatened me on the disastrous repercussions in case I don't listen to him. I took it very casually as it keeps happening in the boys hostel.

'The same evening I thought of visiting Kamna. I inquired about Kamna, but I saw Kamna, Neerja and Meghna coming out of the hostel. As usual, Neerja took the lead and started pulling my leg, "I heard you had gone to attend some marriage. I anticipated if your family might take this as an opportunity and tie your nuptial knot. It's not safe to leave boys alone in today's world."

'I was getting vexed and wanted to be rude with her. I told her, "They would have really considered it, but you were not with me. As you have different interests now, how could they have found a suitable match for me in such a short span."

'"What do you mean by different interests?" Neerja said offensively

'"Neerja has a new boyfriend, Ravi. He threatened and advised me, neither to talk nor to meet you."

'"You are mistaken, he's not my new boyfriend, but my only boyfriend till date and I'm extremely serious about him."

'"Oh! All the best," Neerja got hurt and moved from there, thumping her feet.

'I shifted my focus to Kamna and Meghna, "I apologize for the nasty scene created here. Hi"

'For the first time I heard Meghna saying something, "It's ok. Neerja ma'am seems to be a little disturbed; otherwise, I have never seen her in such a foul mood. Anyways, I'm sorry for you, unnecessarily we have disturbed you. It's my fault, I wanted to accompany Kamna and that's how ma'am also came along with us. She shouldn't have taken so much of liberty with you."

'I realized that she wasn't aware of the relationship between me and Neerja, and that's why she considered her as the culprit. I thought, "If she doesn't have an idea let it be like that."

'I concluded the meeting by saying, "It was no one's fault; some days are just bad." I said bye to them and came back to hostel.

'Meghna, on her side, cried the whole night as she felt I was humiliated, so I might have got disturbed. She even didn't stay in Neerja's room; she shifted to Kamna's cubicle for a night.

'Next day, call from hostel guard woke me up. It would be around 6:00 a.m., I had some visitors and I was shocked to see Kamna and Meghna standing there.

'I asked Kamna, "What's it?"

'She replied helplessly, "Meghna compelled me to come here as she had been crying the whole night."

'I rushed them to my room and closed the door. Meghna was gazing at me.

'I asked her, "Why were you crying?" and she started crying again.

'"Please stop crying; I'll make some tea."

'Meghna felt better. She asked, "How are you?"

'"I'm perfectly fine, but I have still not understood: why did you cry the whole night, and your reason of coming here? Kamna knows I don't like, she or any other girl, visiting this place."

'"I'm sorry, but I was too worried about you after yesterday's incident. I was thinking you might not have taken it to heart so wanted to see you at least once."

'She was melting like an ice and with a wink of eye, she became a super woman. She started cleaning my room. She asked me for a new bed cover; she made my bed .It was apotheosis of my room. She collected all the dirty clothes and asked me for a bag. I told her that washer man would come, but she insisted to wash them. It was little funny, as she was a rich man's daughter who would have never washed her own clothes. But she wanted to do it for me, and that too showing her full command over me.

It was obvious that she was getting involved with me, and she wanted to ensure that I visit her soon.

'This way, I started meeting Meghna. She was an emotional fool but whosoever she was, I found myself totally entrapped in her love. She was so selfless and caring. I eternally wanted to be with her. Whenever I felt little bit stressed, I started rushing to Meghna.

'It was my birthday and I only invited Meghna in a restaurant; although, I got a call from Neerja too, wishing me on the day. We had a lovely evening and when we were about to leave, I jokingly asked her about my gift. She got up from her chair, came closer to my face and kissed me, "How did you find the gift?"

'I blushed, "Nothing like it, but it's too bold."

'"You should never care about others," and we moved out.

'I dropped her to the hostel. I was on top of the world. I knew, "I have found my true love and I'm eager to move forward with my relationship."

Following day, I went to her hostel to collect my clothes. She returned me nicely washed, ironed clothes in my bag. I wasn't sure if it was the right time to ask her about an outdoor trip, but then I mustered all my courage and asked her if she would like to think about such a program.

'The moment I proposed it, she said, "yes", as if it was like a wish comes true for her.

'She added, "I hope Kamna is not accompanying us".

'I derisively said, "I'm thinking about Neerja."

'Before I could even complete my sentence she pounced on me and said, "Don't you even dare to think about her, taking her along with us is a far flung dream?"

'"I'm just joking; it would be only two of us."

'We planned a trip to Simla for two days and one night on coming weekend. I couldn't have afforded more expenses than this. I booked a room at 'Clarks'. It was an expensive hotel. We planned to go by a deluxe bus because that's the most economical and comfortable mode from Delhi. I picked Meghna from her hostel on Saturday, early morning, and around noon we were in Simla. The public was considering us like a married couple. At the hotel reception they greeted Meghna as Ms. Medhansh, and she was thrilled to be addressed by that name. For the next twenty four hours we were locked up in a room. I knew now my life is impossible without her. We didn't realize but the time flew by, and it was the time to get back to our battlefields from this dreamland.

'Sunday, late night; I dropped Meghna back to her hostel. While we were on the gate, I saw Neerja watching us from her window. I noticed her but didn't mention it to Meghna so that she wasn't upset. However in core of my heart I was sure of Neerja not leaving it so easily.

'Now you might call it premonition or I knew Neerja so well, that as soon as Meghna was entering her room, Neerja followed her. Although, internally Meghna had developed some hatred for Neerja but still she regarded her as a senior, and for whatever she had done for her during initial days in the college.

'Neerja asked, "Meghna, where are you coming from?"

'Meghna without mincing any words said, "I was out with Medhansh for two days."

'As anticipated, she didn't like what Meghna told her and she started rebuffing her, "You should have asked me before making any such program."

'What was really offensive for Meghna was that she told her, "He had given me the same proposal around a year back, but I refused."

'Meghna was numb; she felt cheated and robbed by me. She went into her room and cried the whole night. She even didn't care to talk to Kamna about it. I tried calling her the next day but she didn't take my phone. I knew something had happened, so immediately rushed to her hostel. Thanks God! At least she came out. I asked her the reason and she told me everything that had happened on Sunday night. I wanted to kill Neerja for what she did, but then my first priority was to pacify Meghna and tell her the true version. She had developed blind faith in me so whatever I told her she accepted earnestly. However, she had concerns on concealing the truth of Neerja and my relationship from her.

'I told her, "It wasn't a relationship; she's just a friend and that too, due to Kamna." Her face told me that she wasn't convinced.

'My second year was getting over and it was time for summer training, I left for home and so did Meghna. Her summer break had started, and her father was coming to pick her up. She belonged to a filthy rich, conservative Bhumihar Brahmin family. They are usually very staunch people, who would never marry their daughters outside community. Meghna knew about her family but she was very confident of convincing them as she was the only daughter. Anyways, for me, these social norms were irrelevant.

'I got busy in my training for the whole one month. I was doing it religiously as it was the first time and your college reputation is also at stake. I didn't get the time to call Meghna or I was hesitant to call at her home. She also didn't try reaching out to me in any either way, through phone or e-mail. I thought that she was still upset with me, so she was deliberately avoiding me. I wanted to give her time to settle down.

'When we met after our vacations, the moment she saw me she started crying. I took her to a restaurant and thought we would sought out whatever differences we had over a cup of tea. But what she told me was beyond my imagination and a big blow to me;

"I'm engaged," she said

'I cried, "How is it possible?"

'She started narrating me her side of the story, "It was all pre planned. My father came to pick me up from the hostel and there was a guy with him whom I was meeting for the first time. Papa introduced him as Udayveer, son of his childhood friend, who was also studying in Delhi and he was staying near our home. We were to drop him at his place so he was accompanying us in our journey. I was happy; at least, I would have someone to talk to. Udayveer seemed to be a very soft guy who didn't speak much. He was in his final year of MBA and after that he was willing to join his father's business. As he was a quiet guy, I got a chance to speak a lot. I was talking to him all throughout; telling him about girl's college, their hostel, activities, interests etc. For a change, I didn't find my father staring at me with anger, and rather, he was smiling and seemed happy. Usually my Papa doesn't encourage me to talk to guys and that too at this full length. We dropped Udayveer at his home.

'"He asked us to come inside and Papa gave a very zany excuse by saying, "I'll come some other time; she can't come inside right now."

'"I didn't bother to go in between the lines and listened to what he tried telling. It was fine with me. Anyways, I was too tired, I wanted to reach home immediately and meet my mom.

'"My father asked my opinion about Udayveer. He was a nice guy; so without thinking twice, I said all the good things about him. He was glad to hear. I reached home and got busy with my mom. After a week or so, my mom came to me and said that she had something very important to tell me. I was excited to hear it but then when she told me I was shaken to my roots, to know, that they had selected a guy for me and they were planning an engagement ceremony next week. I started crying and wanted to know about the guy.

'""How did you take such a critical decision without seeking my opinion?"

"'My mother said, "We can never think of such a move without your nod.'"

"I'm shocked; and you are telling me that I have given consent!"

"'Mom said, "He is Udayveer, and your father sought your opinion about him.'"

"'I yelled, "It wasn't for the marriage purpose.'"

"'But my mother didn't give much heed to what I said, "You liked him so much and he isn't going to change for the motive. Moreover, in our families parents allow only this extent of meeting and then they decide about the alliance. You are lucky that we have asked your opinion and the fact, you have really liked him." My mom left the room without caring much about anything else. I was crying the whole day, even refused to take any food or water.

"'In the evening, my mother came to me and asked," Meghna, why are you behaving like this?'"

"'I kept crying without uttering a word. Then after a moment I said, "At least, you should have considered about my studies. You know, how much I wanted to complete my graduation.'"

"'She said, "We aren't planning your marriage anytime soon, it's just after his MBA Udayveer is planning to leave for US for further studies and your father wanted some formal announcement before that.'"

"'I told my mother, "In any case, I'm not going to marry him.'"

"'But she sounded too adamant, "There's no alternative as your father has already said yes to them.'"

"'I felt as if I was losing everything, "I'll commit suicide in case you further pressurize me." I anticipated it should work as I'm there only daughter and they'll never like to lose me.

"'My mother left the room in panic. I continued with my hunger strike. It was almost two days since I had taken anything. I felt giddy and started puking. Our maid immediately rushed to my mother and called her. She came in completely zapped and started crying as soon as she saw me in that bedraggled state. She asked our maid to go out of the room. I was sure I had won it. She gave me some water and when I refused to take it, she hugged me and promised to hear my concerns and work on them. I took water as I knew my mom loved me more than anybody else, and would do anything for me. I also love her more than my life, since childhood she has been my only company and I have been for her. I felt a little better and started speaking to her. I told her about you, and our relationship. She kept hearing the memoir and then asked me, "which caste?"

""""Punjabi"

""""Shoo.....family"

""""His father is a business man but not of Papa's stature."

"'I have never seen such infuriated face of my mother till now. She was no more my mother but a wife, and a daughter of bhumihar's.

"'Your father would kill you without blinking his eye even if he heard something like that, and all this crap you had been doing with him. I would have dared to support you if he was from our caste and status. Then also your father would have been brutal with me. Right now, there's no question of even telling him anything. I'm your mother and it's my duty to warn you that your father is going to be real cruel with you in case you do anything wrong. If I tell him now, he would put you under house arrest, and call a doctor and ask him to put you on drip. I beg of you, not to destroy family like this. You are our only hope and we want to see you flourish with Udayveer. Whatever we have is only for you and your father has been working so hard to give you a bright future. Udayveer is a perfect match for you." She left the room crying and came back after two hours to find my condition further deteriorated.

""'Meghna, she hugged me and started crying again. You know my sweet heart I can't do anything about it, even I can't call a doctor as your father would come to know about the truth and you won't be allowed to even complete your graduation. If you don't yield, you are going to die and in any case I won't be able to live."

"'She got hysterical and said, "I'm giving you another hour to think about it and become normal otherwise I'm going to take away my life; at least I won't be there to see whatever happens afterwards."

"'Once more I knew she was telling the truth as my grandmother committed suicide when my maternal uncle married his love outside our clan."

'Meghna started crying loudly in the restaurant and held my hands firmly, "*At that moment I realized, I can't be so selfish to destroy her life for my love. Medhansh, I'm sorry I have ruined your life. I tried my best but couldn't do anything for it. Promise me, you will be the same person with me for the next two years, till the time they marry me; then you are free to go anywhere. Consider from this moment we are married and I'm going to die after two years. Marry anyone after that but never forget me, keep me in your heart forever.*"

'It was getting too heavy and complex for me. I wanted to run away from there. My all dreams were shattered; I loved Meghna and thought she was my soul mate. There were several questions surfacing my mind, but I wanted all of them to be kept aside for now. I dropped Meghna back to her hostel.

'I was so upset that I wasn't able to concentrate on my studies properly. One day, I was lost somewhere in the class and my professor asked me a question. I was like a dead pan. It was so embarrassing. Professor asked me to leave the class and come back, once all my problems were resolved, and I would be in a state to focus. I got afraid, this way I might not flunk in my degree. It would have been a great setback for my parents. My mother has really worked hard on me and in no way I could have disappointed them. I told myself, "I'll have to compromise with my fate and forget Meghna."

'But Meghna would have never allowed me to forget her. She called me once and said that she would jump from her hostel building if I don't reach to her within half an hour. I immediately rushed to her and she was standing there on the gate waiting for me. She had stopped caring for people now, as soon as she saw me, she ran towards me and hugged me.

'"Why didn't you come for so many days to see me?"

'I said, "I'm a little busy with my studies."

'"You don't know how to lie; you are trying to avoid me. Let me clarify one thing to you: you are mine for the next two years."

'I didn't understand whether Meghna loved me or if she was just being selfish. It appeared only love to me that she wanted to live her whole life with me in these two years. I agreed to whatever she said and decided to be with her for the next two years. I found it a convenient solution at the time. And who knows? Some twist of fate might present itself within that time which would extend our relationship permanently. So I promised to meet her every other day and resolved to concentrate on Meghna and my studies for now. Life started showering peace on me. Meanwhile, news of Neerja getting engaged reached everyone's ears. In spite of this new relationship being undesirable to her, still she wanted to be loyal to it by wearing an engagement ring.

'Neerja rang me and asked for a tete-a-tete the next day in our famous Deer park. I declined to meet her. She then instigating me said, "Is it due to the fear of Ravi that you don't want to see me?"

'My male ego had been challenged and I asked her the time when she wanted to meet. She said, "5 o'clock". The next day, I was there at the appointed time. She came on time, wearing a white suit and diamond earrings. She looked like a white rose with dew drops sparkling on it. I ignored her beauty and straightaway asked her the purpose of this meeting. She said she wanted to console me for whatever had happened in my life.

'She was about to say something more when I saw Ravi and a few of his guys coming towards me with rods in their hands. Ravi pushed Neerja out of the way and his goons started beating me till every bone in my body cracked. I could hear Neerja crying to stop it but they didn't halt, and finally when I was very nearly dead, they left the place. Neerja rushed me to a nearby hospital where I was admitted to the intensive care unit. Later as the situation stabilized and by evening I was shifted to a private room. Both Neerja and Meghna were with me. They were friends again.

'As soon as I recovered, I started meeting Meghna every other day. Neerja felt guilty for the incident so she never met me after that. I came to know in my hostel that she broke off with Ravi as well. Meghna and I were going out the same way as if nothing had happened. Meghna wanted to visit Simla, 'Clarks', before the end of our lives. I had stopped being realistic and wanted to ensure that her every wish was fulfilled at any cost. We went back to Simla, this time for a longer duration. I could see the impact of this emotional web on my studies. I was getting more and more entwined with every passing day. I ended my third year with very average grades. I recognized, "Meghna is going to be there with me for another year and if this continues, I, for sure, shall muck up my whole degree. I'm now even ready to put my graduation at stake. For me everything is fair in love and war. But I'm perplexed, whether I love her or is it a war which I'm fighting with myself."

'Summer break was the time to part with Meghna. We promised to be in touch with each other, whatever the case may be. That was the last time I saw or spoke to her. I tried calling at her home but no one picked up the phone. I wrote her e-mails but everyone bounced back. Kamna told me that her parents had decided to get her married that very month. Apparently, in addition to her mother knowing of our relationship, now her father came to know of it. They got their land line disconnected and told Meghna to close her e-mail account. There was no way she could have contacted me. Kamna went to her wedding and shared with me, "Everything went well and she isn't going to come back to complete her graduation." Our love story came to a grief-stricken end. In the beginning I was down in the dumps, but then time is a big healer and life takes its own course. Today, I'm sitting here alive in front of you and life goes on.'

'Oh, food is here,' Sara said coming back to the present moment. She had become very involved in Medhansh's saga and her face showed that she was sympathetic towards him.

They finished their food and Sara coined it as a taxing dinner. Medhansh dropped Sara back home. It was late but then it was okay as now Sara was grown up and knew how to manage herself. Diya too had returned by that time. It was a tiring day for both of them, so they didn't talk much and went to sleep.

After that she wasn't like her real self for many days. She sensed that a stone had been tied on to her head and she was always brooding about Medhansh's topsy-turvy past life which had raised many questions with no answers.

CHAPTER 7

*M*EDHANSH CALLED UP SARA the next day and asked her if she was fine. He apologized to her for burdening her with his Eeyorish reminiscence. Sara was feeling sorry for Medhansh and wanted to say a few soothing words. But before she could say a word he said, 'Sara, I haven't shared with you the biggest blunder of my life which I committed after losing Meghna.'

Sara got inquisitive, 'What's that?'

Medhansh continued, 'I still kept in regular contact with Kamna after Meghna had left the hostel. Once in a while Neerja used to be with Kamna and we started interacting again. I was grief stricken, so Neerja became a source of emotional support for me. Her presence always refreshed me.

'One day I became so daring that I thought of going to Neerja's room in the girl's hostel. Neerja had once invited me to her room and I had left it for some other time. I thought it was the time to fulfill the promise. I jumped the hostel boundary and moved towards the main building. It was late at night so nobody saw me. Hostel guards are humans too; they believe in almighty and prefer to leave everything to God at this hour and go to sleep. I had an idea, Neerja's cubicle was on second floor and her room's window opened towards the lawn side. I started climbing up the water conduit and safely reached outside her window. The lights were still on and she was reading a book while sitting in a chair. I called her name twice, Neerja....Neerja. She got discombobulated and rushed towards the window to find me flapping outside it. She opened the window and gave me her hand through the window grill and pulled me onto the window extension on which I was dangling. Once inside, Neerja prepared tea for me and we talked until dawn. It was risky to stay there any longer, so I bid her good-bye with a morning kiss and hurriedly left for my hostel. I was happy that I had moved on in my life and had found my lost love that always stood by me through thick and thin. We kept meeting in the same way for six months. My scholastic life had started improving. Again, I was winner of the numbers race being played in every academic institution. My seventh semester GP was among the highest. I regained my respect and confidence. Zest for life had started creeping into me again. I had started loving myself more than ever.

'I thought it's high time I should take an initiative and move to the next step. I invited her to a restaurant and proposed to her. She was dispassionate, as if she had had a hunch it was coming.

'I asked her to say something and what she said was what I'd anticipated.'

'"Medhansh, candidly I could read this in your eyes a while back and I had anticipated this proposal coming but wished it wouldn't have happened. You are aware, I'm from a family of landlords and you belong to a middle class business family. I'm also apprehensive of your future prospects, as chemical engineering is not considered to hold a great potential. Please excuse me, Medhansh, for being so blunt. It's a fact I like you but that doesn't mean I'm ready to play with my life. I'm looking for a stable partner with handsome earnings who can give me every comfort of life. *This life is very short and I'm unenthusiastic about spending it struggling. Love is an ornament of the affluent, there can be no love if you need to fight for your existence.* We are good friends and shall always stay so. I can't think of a long term relationship unless you are well settled. I hope till then my parents don't tie my knot with someone else."

'I told her, "You are humiliating me, it sounds as if she you are making a business proposal of my emotions."

'She laughed at me and said, "Business proposal of your emotions! Where your emotions were when you were going around with me and at the same time started flirting with Meghna? I too felt humiliated."

'I had started cracking from inside. I realized the venom she carried in her heart and as an afterthought I felt perhaps that she could very well have been the one to inform of our alliance to Meghna's dad. It was just my hunch.

'I told her, "I saw you falling for Ravi so I didn't have any choice but to move out of the relationship."

'Neerja was sarcastic, "You hardly broke off with me, and the next day you were in love with someone else. Were you running in a marathon? You should have at least given yourself some time and sought clarity from me." I knew at that moment, that it was an unsalvageable relationship. I had made a buffoon of myself by exposing my feelings.

'From the time she became cognizant of my pay package, her interest in me has revived. But you commit a mistake once in life and not every time.'

Sara was only more confused after listening to Medhansh. She was unable to analyze the whole set of circumstances and form opinion. One fact was obvious in Sara's mind, "*Love happens once in a lifetime and it can't be love again; it can be liking, convenience or even compatibility.*"

Medhansh wanted to know Sara's innermost thoughts. She diverted the conversation. 'Is it going to change anyone's life? If no, then why should we discuss such an irrelevant issue?'

Medhansh said, 'Yes Sara, it's going to change my life. I value your opinion, apart from being intelligent you are a sensitive girl, and moreover it can help me release my guilt which I'm carrying till now.'

'So, in this case we need to meet over a cup of black coffee and Pepsi sometime next week.'

'Can't you make it this week? I'm eager to hear you.'

'Okay, How about day after tomorrow at Dragon restaurant?'

Both of them met at Dragon's restaurant.

'Hi, hope it wasn't too uncomfortable for you to come today,' Medhansh said.

'Nope, today I'm idle. My college is starting after few days.' Sara wanted to drop a hint to Medhansh that she might not be able to spare time for him once she joins back. 'When are you joining your job?'

'Next week.'

'So we'll be getting involved with our works at the same time,' Sara said.

'Which stream will you opt for?' asked Medhansh.

'Finance and IT.'

'Good combination!'

'Ya!' Sara wanted to get down to the business at hand. 'Tell me, why have you called me here?'

'I told you, to seek your opinion....'

'If you want me to say soothing words, I can say that anyways. You don't need my opinion for that.'

'Nope, I wanna hear your opinion,' Sara's sixth sense told her, "things are getting messy and now he is trying his luck with me."

'I might sound rude.' she said finally.

'I can take it,' Medhansh said.

'Well, if you want my feelings, I'd say there was no true love anywhere.'

Medhansh considered the statement for a moment, and then nodded slightly.

She continued, 'It was just lust or you can say in this age you are eager to be with someone for no good reason.'

Medhansh asked inquisitively, 'Why do you think so?'

'In my opinion, *love is like permanent glue which sticks two souls and they can't be separated unless they are lacerated. Souls are immortal and so is love.* Love is more than a biochemical reaction between two people. It might sound philosophical, but I consider two people can love each other without weighing any attributes and the feeling is so selfless that you always want to see the other person happy. It's an emotion so strong that two people talk to one another without using any words or any other form of expression. Their feelings are, as if they are waves travelling between two hearts. It's something which you can feel but can never see, like a cool breeze. You just realize that you are connected with something unseen. If you love someone, you hear the unheard.

'In your scenario, both Meghna and Neerja were self-centered and were satisfying their egos through you. It's obvious from your talk that Neerja was flirting with you to have a gala time at college. She had a preconceived image of her partner and you were never a match to that. Anyways, for her, love was material. If I leave that aside, I must say she portrayed a strong-willed girl, who fancied certain attributes in her companion and she frankly shared it with you. Your feelings for her were mere infatuation; otherwise, there was no question of Meghna coming in between both of you. In short it was a relationship without much foundation.

'Meghna, on the other hand, was a lily-livered personality. She was coming from a conservative family where limited freedom is given to girls. She had a dominating father and a submissive mother. The moment she was in a free environment, and she met a soft and caring man like you, she started filling voids in her life.

'Her insecurity took the shape of authority on you, which guys like you are crazy about, especially before marriage. When she was getting into a relationship with you, she was conscious that it would be an uphill task and, in spite of that, she took it forward without ensuring to herself the sacrifices it might involve. She was totally wrapped up in herself and never gave a damn about your feelings and neither did you as you showed by going back to her friend.'

Sara smirked, 'You three had a nice two years of your life.'

Medhansh was like a frozen chick after listening to Sara's opinion. He had a notion that Sara carried a traditional mindset and was rigid in her thinking; he found no chance of entering into a relationship with her.

Silence prevailed for a moment as Medhansh sighed heavily and ordered black coffee for Sara and tea for him. Sara could see the doleful expression visible on Medhansh's face. To ease it a bit she giggled and said, 'Medhansh, you didn't check on my preference for coffee this time.'

Lost in his own world Medhansh said, 'I wish if it wasn't black coffee you can change it to cold coffee.'

Sara laughed. 'Why, do you want to change my choice?'

'No, sorry,' he replied with an unconvincing smile. 'I was thinking something else. Black coffee is the best choice.'

They had their coffee and tea, and neither of them uttered a word. When they were done they said their good-byes and parted.

Sara wasn't as composed internally as she was showing outside, after all she was a female; emotions were flowing in her veins. She wanted to cry for Medhansh. Deep in her heart Sara felt, "It's just that he is an emotional boy, so both the girls exploited him. His feelings were true and he did the whole lot to prove his liking apart from a few blips. Then, to err is human. But the very fact he moved on means there was no spiritual connection between them."

Medhansh was worried about his sharing of everything with Sara. Sara's philosophy of love and liking didn't convince him but at the moment he realized just one thing, he couldn't live without Sara. He was crystal clear in his thinking about it. "Sara is the best partner I can ever have. I'm fascinated by her independent spirit." At the moment, Medhansh was too scared to express his emotions to Sara. He had already revealed everything of his inglorious past and besides, her idiosyncratic notion of love was a Damoclesean sword hanging over his life.

In any case, there wasn't any ambiguity in Medhansh's mind. "Life gives you such a chance only once and only those who are ready to sacrifice their lives to avail themselves of the opportunity emerge as the winner." He was determined to propose to her one day. Medhansh was a seasoned guy; he knew he'd have to take the opportunity before she joined college to pursue her MBA degree. He was afraid of the many options that would be available to her at school and God knows which one might ring a bell of love... love...in her heart. Before that could happen, he wanted to knock at her door.

Medhansh called up Sara the next day. 'Hi, how are you?'

'Just fine.' she said. 'Enjoying a last few days of stay with my family. How's life treating you?'

Avoiding an answer, he said, 'Can we meet before you start for your college?'

'I wish I could but I don't think it's workable this time. I want to spend time with my family.'

'I appreciate your emotions, but can you please just gimme one more evening of your life? I'm aware, I have already bothered you a lot but this last time, please do this favor for me.'

She was silent while she considered the request. 'You haven't left me with any choice, Medhansh! Okay, I shall come.'

She often didn't know how to say 'no' even if she direly needed to do so. This was a weakness to her personality which she felt she needed to work on.

They met at the Dragon restaurant again. Medhansh knew this was the last chance and he had come prepared for it. They took the table reserved for them. This time, Medhansh wanted nothing to be left to destiny. He desired to control it.

'What will you prefer to drink?'

'You know its black coffee.'

Medhansh ordered two black coffees. He didn't want to show any difference in their liking.

'Sara, without mincing any words, I wanna tell you, I wish to spend rest of my life with you. I have gone through a bitter and painful experience of love or liking, whatever you may call it, and now I want a long-lasting committed relationship based on mutual trust and care. Someone to whom I can dedicate my life to, and I feel you are the one for me. Will you be my life partner?'

This came as a surprise to Sara. She didn't explode as she often did; she knew Medhansh was heartbroken twice. Instead, she politely said, 'Medhansh, you are a very nice guy, but please don't get me wrong. I don't want to enter into any relationship. Marriage is not my cup of tea. I want to focus on my career for the time.' For a moment her heart cried and she wished that Sidhant could have proposed to her instead.

Medhansh was encouraged to find her not going hysterical. He was better confident now rest he can handle.

'Sorry I'm such a big fool, I never asked you if you are dating someone. I am sure he will be gem of a person and the luckiest man on this earth. It's my mistake; I never imagined that you can be involved with someone.'

Sara stared at him.

'No, no! I don't mean you can't be involved, for you there will be countless guys and I will be standing nowhere. I meant everyone would have dreaded to think of it, as you don't look like to be a soft hearted person with opposite sex.

'Moreover you have confined love with in so many boundaries I find it impossible for you to get enchanted by anyone.'

'And for you love is like air, omnipresent,' Sara frowned over his last remark.'

"I'm not saying it happens now and then but it could be situational. You are true at your place but circumstances drag you to a corner, and your relationship comes to an end. *If your heart beats and mind thinks then you are bound to get green light.*" Medhansh never wanted to be more assertive than this, and hurt Sara.

'We can agree to disagree'

'Yes ma'am as you say, but I started with something very different and I'm still awaiting your reply'

'Medhansh, you are a nice guy.

Pause.................

'I don't even believe in dating, you accept a person as is and then love him or her for what he or she is. Love doesn't come after matching compatibility; it's a deep internal feeling not swayed by superficial things. It doesn't mean I'm saying that I don't like you, it's just I have never thought of it as I'm not keen to enter into this institution right now...............

'I have never said you can't marry someone if you only like him and not love him. To be honest with you, I don't think I can love anyone, yes I can be a life partner but not right now.'

Medhansh knew she was withholding something; otherwise, love is not such a complex thing that someone is so averse to it. He preferred to stay quiet and wait for the right moment.

'Sara, I'm ready to wait lifelong for you. I can't think about anyone else ever since I met you, so if you call it love then I'm deeply in love with you and my life will stop if you say *no*.'

Sara smiled; Medhansh didn't sound convincing to her. His words were devoid of any feeling or conviction. She never felt that passion in him. Anyways her intent was never to hurt someone and make herself happy by feeling that she has got the true love when she wasn't patronizing the same feelings. On the other hand she was also clear that she liked Medhansh for his simplicity, guileless and caring nature.

'I can commit you one thing that if ever in my life I think of entering into a relationship you will be my only life partner.'

Sara further added teasingly, 'Subject to you are single at that time.'

Medhansh was thinking, "She is a big idiot if she ever thinks I'll let her go without a commitment."

Now he knew well, 'She is a sweet kid who is happy living in her own wonder world of philosophies and if he wants to be with her, he'll have to start speaking her language as kids better understand their own language.'

'I'll wait, but I'll keep knocking your door from time to time for your reply.' Medhansh accompanied Sara in her car till her home and then took a bus from there.

Life was becoming complex for Sara. She wanted to say *no* to Medhansh but couldn't hurt him as he was twice traumatized in the past. When she thought of him she felt good for whoever he was, but memories of Sidhant used to flash back in her mind and she used to start feeling guilty as if she had done something wrong with him. It was getting simply bewildering for Sara. She had hardly spoken to Sidhant but the kind of queasiness even his thought was creating in her mind and soul was beyond her understanding.

20th March, 2010: Medhansh was to leave for Hyderabad to join his new job.

He called up Sara, 'Can you please come to the airport to meet me?'

Sara knew she won't go but again she found it difficult to say *no*.

'I'll try my best but can't commit.'

'Anyways, my eyes will be only looking for you. Bye'

'Bye'

Medhansh was sure, 'She'll come.'

He wanted to be alone with her before he leaves, so he asked his family not to come with him to the airport as he was to pick up a friend on the way. Medhansh was so perturbed that he reached the Indira Gandhi International Airport at 6:30 a.m., one hour earlier to the scheduled time .He was flying by British Airways. He stood outside Gate No. 2, waiting for Sara to arrive. His restlessness was growing with passing time. He turned his face towards every car coming there. He started moving back and forth and his pace was increasing with every minute gone. Sara didn't turn up and he stood there, even he was late by 2 hours to his reporting time. Then, he called her up.

Sara picked up the phone and informed him her inability to come due to ill health.

Medhansh knew, 'Sara, you are trying to avoid me and I'm not hurt. If you find it ok, can you please share the reason with me? If you aren't comfortable I won't insist. I want to request you only one thing, "Consider me a human being who can't even imagine existing without you, and then make a decision. If my past is something that's bothering you, I swear it was a mistake. The way I feel about you, I haven't ever felt in my life. I'm conscious you like me and I can assure you after sometime you are going to love me.'

Sara was too touched, she wanted to assuage Medhansh in every possible way but still she wasn't ready to accept any feelings beyond liking for him. 'Medhansh you are embarrassing me. You aren't aware of your worth; you deserve someone much better than me.'

'I don't care about anyone else, you are the best and if you aren't accepting me, this world is useless for me.

Sara, if you want me to go and work for our future you'll have to say *yes* to me otherwise I'm not going. Without you I'll just want to end my journey of life in a desolated place because I'm such a big looser. I have a few minutes left, if I don't enter now I'll miss the flight. Decision will be yours; I'm waiting for your answer.'

Medhansh was creating undue pressure on Sara without realizing, love is not just entering into a relationship as if sowing a seed. But it's about nurturing your relationship with selfless care, honesty, sincerity, passion and respect for it to exist and flourish.

Sara was falling short of words. With lot of efforts she said, 'Medhansh there was a guy in my life. He's always in my mind; although, I'm never clear about my feelings for him.'

Medhansh jumped the gun and said, 'No it's nothing, you are an emotional girl so you get concerned about everyone. Trust me when we are together you won't remember anything. It will be just two of us. I can hear my name being announced, this is the final call, say, *yes.*'

There was so much of pressure on Sara's mind and she had no time to deliberate. In impulse she said, 'yes.'

Medhansh said, 'I love you,' and hung up the phone. He rushed towards the entrance and not by any chance he could have missed this opportunity, everything in his life was going as per his whims.

"God destines whatever is best for you. May be, Medhansh's relationships in the past were not successful, because he is destined for me. He is a simple guy; I'm sure, he'll always understand me and be with me in every walk of life." She was lost in her thoughts and suddenly her phone buzzed.

'Hi Sara, I have reached Hyderabad. I wanna talk to you as soon as I reach.'

Sara was glad to be someone's first, 'Good, I was contemplating about you since you left'

'I'm on top of the world! You have started spending time with me. I'm sure after sometime you will like to spend whole of your life with me'

'It's ok; don't try to get romantic every time......'

'Oh my God! She's still the same,' Medhansh laughed

'Please focus on your job now. First few days are very important as they create a long term impression, and don't waste too much of your time and money in calling me'

'I won't waste, it's an investment and ma'am you can't stop me from that'

'Ok, bye for now,' Sara asked Medhansh to disconnect the phone as she never wanted him to be extravagant.

CHAPTER 8

SARA JOINED HER NEW college.

She was coming with an avid desire to learn the art of minting money and controlling its supply. There were students from different streams of art, commerce, economics, and Sara was relishing this vivid experience. She got too busy in her assignments and case studies that she didn't find enough time to go back home. Once in a while she used to get phone from Medhansh and after every phone she was apprehensive over her choice. Neither were they soul mates nor earthly mates, as neither Sara felt strongly for him nor they were aligned in their outlook towards life. It was simply Sara's sympathetic attitude and commitment she had made to Medhansh, she was trying to make this relationship work.

One day, to her surprise she received a call from Rohit; Jimmy and he were coming to see her in the college. Sara kept wondering, "Why were they coming?" She started waiting for them. They reached her hostel in the evening. Sara made them sit in the visitor's room.

'Hi Sara,' Rohit and Jimmy said.

'Hi Rohit, hi Jimmy; long time all well,'

There was a pin drop silence in the room for few minutes as no one could figure out from where to start. Sara found the whole environment very uncomfortable.

She took the lead and started talking to Jimmy, 'How's your college going?'

'Fine, but not as interesting as B.Tech'

'How's Avni?'

Jimmy blushed for a while and then said, 'Avni is doing very fine but she misses your company a lot.'

'Why does she needs me now, you are there, what else she wants?' Sara said jovially

Jimmy in a submissive voice said, 'Very soon you might get our wedding invitation.'

'Come on! Are you joking?' Sara questioned.

'It's true; Avni parents want it that way.'

'Or Avni wants to be sure that you don't fly away anywhere' Sara said laughing. Jimmy and Rohit were little surprised to find Sara talking to them so coolly about something which used to be a big taboo for her.

'What about you Rohit? How are you finding your job?'

'No tensions, I'm enjoying it'

'So you are settled now, have you found some girl for you or still trying?'

'Neither I have found anyone nor I'm trying. This should be better left to parents as they best understand you, and fact of the matter is in our society it's not only the marriage of a girl and a boy but two families marry each other. So for a happy married life it's better left to them.'

'Interesting,' Sara said; but within herself she was confounded on vicissitude of his thoughts. She felt responsible for the change in Rohit.

They kept discussing about the whole batch, Sara was still not clear of their purpose of coming there. But as usual she couldn't control herself and asked about Sidhant,

'What Sidhant is doing nowadays?'

'He has left his job at Bangalore,' Rohit said as if he was waiting for this question to come up.

'Why? What does he plan to do now?' Sara said looking at both of them. Sara was not astonished as she considered it to be very much expected from him.

'Next month he's flying to the U.S, he has made it to a top management school there,' Jimmy said with sparkles of appreciation in his eyes.

'It's wonderful!' Sara said with mixed feelings. She was really enthused. This was little more than what she had expected from Sidhant; although, she had never doubted his capabilities. There was no reason for being so confident about him but she never understood why she was always so optimistic about him. On the other hand she was upset for herself as she wasn't able to even clear IIMs although she had put in her best.

'Sara, tell us something about you. How's your new life?' Rohit asked.

'I'm fine; nothing has changed,' before she could complete herself...

Jimmy barged in to add, 'Except you have gained some weight!'

Sara laughed and said, 'Jimmy, I'll be conscious from now onwards'

Sara took them to a nearby restaurant. They had some nice time over a cup of tea refreshing memorable time they all had spent together. She, out of courtesy, took their contact numbers and asked them to stay in touch. After sometime they bid good-bye to Sara and left the place.

As Sara was apprehensive about Sidhant's sentiments for her, so was he. He fell for Sara but was afraid of being dumped by her, so he never took a chance to express himself. The metamorphosis of Sidhant was a testimony of his love for Sara. Unfortunate part of life was, *both of them considered love beyond words yet they waited for each other to say something.* He always found himself up the creek without a paddle in front of her, it was impossible for him to say her anything.

They were gone; however, for days to come Sara kept wondering the reason of their visit. She was surprised that they were never so close pals that within few months of separation they would visit to check on her well being. Worst she could reflect was, Sidhant wanted to show her down by telling her of his achievement, so he asked them to visit her. She considered that she had hurt his male ego by not being polite to him but that was due to his irksome behavior; whereas, he might have felt, she gave a damn to him because of his erratic behavior and future prospects.

Sara was baffled, "If her thoughts, has an iota of truth, then someone should tell him- there's no co relation between love and future prospects! There is an old saying 'love is blind', and then also we don't understand that blind love can never look for anything. What an irony?"

Internally it was a very tough moment for Sara to have Sidhant's memories refreshed in her mind once he was out of her life. She was so disquiet that she called up Medhansh and told him everything, while she was narrating the whole incident her voice got choked, Medhansh could feel tears in her eyes, and with heavy voice she said,' Medhansh we should rethink about our relationship. His thought has made me so nostalgic as if he's still vacillating somewhere in my mind and I'm not sure if I'll be able to do justice to our relationship. I know he could have sent them with all the negative intentions of hurting me but still I don't understand why I am so upset?'

Medhansh after listening to Sara got insecure, he was now having a better feel of her emotions, "there's something more than a passing reference between them; guy like Sidhant, wouldn't have cared to hurt Sara. It was a commendable achievement for him. As old saying goes 'Behind every successful man there's a woman', and this time, it was Sara who was behind him." Medhansh was sure, at any cost he won't let this feeling set in Sara as she was indispensable for him, he would die without her.

Medhansh consoled Sara and tried to convince her that she was doleful because she couldn't tolerate an insouciant person achieving so much whereas she had to compromise on her aspirations. Sara never wanted to believe this reason but this much charisma he had created on her that after listening to him she started pacifying herself.

I'm planning to visit you next week. I'm short of time, so I won't go home; I'll spend a day with you,' Medhansh said.

Innocent Sara, she started working on his stay arrangements. The moment he confirmed that he was coming, she got him booked in faculty guest house for a day, without even asking him. When Medhansh arrived he proposed her an outstation trip. It was shocking for Sara.

"What'll I tell to my parents, and how can I go without informing them?" Sara told to herself

'No Medhansh I don't want to deceive my parents. I don't think I'm prepared for it.'

'Who's asking you to deceive them, inform them that you are going out with me for two days? They know me very well.'

'What? You mean to say I inform my father about it and he would gladly allow me to enjoy my two days with you. Come on! I'm from a very traditional family. I can never dare to ask them such a freakish thing.'

'When you are intelligent enough to understand that they won't like it; then you shouldn't at first place raise this concern of informing them. You are grown up now and should know these decisions are situational and there's nothing like, "cheating your parents". Moreover, we are committed to each other.'

'No more justifications, it's not possible. If you want to stay here for a night I have got you booked in guest house, otherwise you can plan to leave back by evening or go and visit your parents.'

Medhansh knew it was of no use to argue with her at this time. He reminded himself of the purpose of his visit, to wipe out Sidhant from her mind and if she takes something negatively about him she would start chanting Sidhant's name again.

'I'm here to make you happy. Whatever you say I'm fine with it,' Medhansh said blithely but with a bleeding heart.

She accompanied him to the guest house so that he can freshen up. For the first time Sara realized that Medhansh is preparing to create new boundaries. As soon as they entered the room he shut the door and pressed her to the wall engulfing her in his arms and kissed her. Sara was shocked at his behavior but then tried to loosen her mind a bit so she didn't scream at him. She pushed him back and said, 'Enough of romance, get ready and come out. I'm waiting for you at the reception.' She moved out without giving him a look. Medhansh kept wondering,' Was this enough of romancing? Does she even understand what romance is? My God! It's my turn now to think whether she is the right choice. I hope, I don't waste half or even complete life, explaining her that s-e-x is not a crime.'

Medhansh got freshened up. He sprayed some Noir on him expecting it to do some wonders. He moved out to flatter her lady. She was sitting outside anxiously waiting for him. Anxiousness was not because she was dying to meet him but she wanted to take him out of the campus as soon as possible so that nobody sees him with her, and her image of Ms Professional shouldn't be impacted. Sara had a pre conceived notion that girls going around with someone in the college aren't taken in a good light by their professors.

It was lunch time. They decided to go to Delhi Darbar, Connaught Place, to have their lunch. They were going without reservation so it took them more than half an hour to grab a table for themselves. They were so hungry by that time, food was their first priority. Sara was a non-vegetarian so she preferred to order butter chicken and Naan. Medhansh was like a cute Mamma's son who preferred lentils and cheese. While they were waiting for their order Sara casually asked Medhansh about his family.

'I have given you such a big commitment and have never asked you about your family. I'm sorry for my lackadaisical attitude. But now I feel, at least I should know about them, they are going to be important part of my life.'

'No I don't think it's going to make any change if you don't know them. Anyways, we aren't going to stay with them and for whatever time you meet them, I'm sure you are smart enough to make them happy.'

'Look, I'm not here to make anybody happy. These relationships are of mutual respect and love. If they are good to me, I'll be extremely good to them.'

'Don't worry; they'll be very loving.'

CHAPTER 9

'*B*UT, STILL YOU HAVEN'T told me about your family.'

'My mother is nucleus of my family. She's an educated and independent woman who preferred to be a house wife. She has raised us with care and love.'

Sara interrupted in between, 'No wonder every mother does that.'

'She's a special lady; she used to be awake and sitting with me till dawn while I was preparing for my competitions. I was unable to study, always required someone by my side.'

'I'm sure, she must be a great lady, but on a lighter note, you are a clumsy guy.' Medhansh preferred to ignore it.

Medhansh had some strong positives. His optimism and unflappable nature made him special. Although, he was optimistic in every aspect of life, but this time he was getting over optimistic for Sara by ignoring the contrasting personalities of both of them. Sara was a matter of fact person. She would call an apple- an apple and a mango- a mango, whereas, Medhansh was ready to call an apple- a pineapple if it pleased someone and helped his goal. He was too much bothered about hurting anyone's feelings, and that's why for Sara he was too cheesy.

'I have three siblings; one elder brother and two younger sisters. My elder brother, Mohit, is not very educated as he wasn't good at studies since childhood. He is involved in our family business. He is married to his love, Supriya. She isn't our caste but my parents are very liberal.'

'Why do you say your parents are very liberal, her parents would also be liberal, that's why they have allowed her to marry your brother? Don't you think you are too much obsessed by greatness of your parents?'

'She eloped with my brother. Till date, her parents are not happy with this marriage, and suggest her to leave my brother and come back.'

'Why is it so?'

'They are filthy rich and they don't find our family befitting their status; neither have they held a good opinion about my brother-his educational background and dependency on my father for his finances.'

'So, what if Supriya leaves your brother?'

'She's little dud but she loves my brother. I don't think for materialistic things she's going to leave him anytime.'

'That's good!'

'I have two sisters, Nina is the elder one and Tina is the youngest. Nina completed her graduation last year. We are looking for a suitable match for her, and the day that search is over she would be married.'

'Is she not pursuing higher studies or she's also not good at studies?' Sara said

'My parents don't want girls to study a lot. They think girls should be able to manage their home front well.'

'How did you then think about me?'

'It's their opinion not mine. I like intelligent professional girls.'

'But, neither of your X-girlfriends was intelligent or professional. Are you clear about yourself?'

'What are you trying to do, Sara? Are you pulling my leg?' Medhansh said, trying to make things light.

'No, they are already too long. I don't want to waste my energies on futile things. I'm just trying to understand you better.'

'My younger sister is in second year B.Com,' Medhansh was quiet after that.

'What about your father?'

'He's a business man, brass exporter. He started with a very small base, but now he is quite established.'

After listening to Medhansh, Sara felt quite uneasy. She knew her parents won't like his family background. It's not that her parents gave importance to financial status of a family, but as they were professionals they would have preferred professionals like them, well-educated with a progressive mindset. However, Sara was sure; they won't stop her from taking her decision in life because they had full faith in her.

Medhansh could see that stress on Sara's face, so he asked her, 'Is there something troubling you?'

'Yes, I'm skeptical about my parent's reaction on your family background?'

'What's wrong in it?'

'Nothing, it's only that we seem to be coming from culturally different backgrounds.'

Medhansh knew Sara was right in her observation, but he always had a myopic view about the things, and considered time as the biggest solution provider for every problem.

'I don't think it's important. I love you and you love me, rest everything is immaterial.'

'I'm committed to you; Sara clarified her feelings once again, as if she was the God mother of honesty.'

'Whatever,' Medhansh said, taking it in a spirit.

'Oh, food is here! I'm very hungry.'

Sara had lost her appetite by that time. Something in her subconscious mind was troubling her. She was going ahead with the idea of being Medhansh's life partner but somehow there was a conflict going on between her mind and heart. Her heart always took her to Sidhant but her mind always negated Sidhant; she wasn't even sure what Sidhant thought about her. Mind always supported Medhansh as he was a cool headed, emotional and caring guy.

Moreover, by now, Sara has started believing that there's nothing like *blind love* in this world; otherwise, she would have realized her feelings about Sidhant and he would have reciprocated the same.

They finished their lunch and moved out. Medhansh was aware that Sara wasn't feeling too comfortable. To divert her attention and to make her happy he suggested her to indulge in some shopping. He knew shopping is every girl's weakness so he dragged her to a jeans store. He bought a Calvin Klein jeans and a weekender top for her. Sara refused to take it, as it was an expensive gift, and her parents wouldn't have liked it if she took it back home.

Medhansh suggested, 'Hide it from them, after an age you need not tell them everything.'

'That's why I said, there's a culture difference among our families. We are a close knitted family. My parents have given full freedom to me and in return, at least, I can respect their likes and dislikes. I do few things, and can't do anything about them even if they don't like, as I also have a mind of my own, but for rest of them I can be sensitive to their feelings.'

It was too much of philosophy for Medhansh, which was beyond his understanding. He just wanted every moment to be pleasant, whether by hook or crook.

Medhansh twisted the talk, 'You'll have to take it; when I told my mother about you and our future plans, she asked me to buy a gift for you. Take it as a token of blessings from her.'

Sara was left with no choice but to accept it. She knew, she was going to show it to her mother, as the first thing when she goes back.

It was late in the evening and Sara expressed her desire to go back to her hostel. Sara went back to her hostel and Medhansh, with heavy heart, to campus guest house. Medhansh couldn't sleep for a moment. Whole night he was thinking that Sara was with him, and he was making love to her. He was desperate to feel Sara.

Medhansh was ready early in the morning, as that's what they had planned- to meet as soon as possible. By afternoon, he had to catch his flight.

The day went fine; majority of the time they were making future plans.

Medhansh went back to Hyderabad and Sara got involved in her routine.

That week end; she decided to go home. She took Medhansh's gift along with her, untouched, in the same hand bag. When her mother was alone in the room she kept it on the table.

Her mother asked her, 'What's in the bag?' She took out a pair of jeans and a pink colored top.

Looking at it, she said, 'Sara, this is awesome! It seems expensive. Who gave you the money to buy all this? I haven't given you anything.'

She laughed, 'I'm sure you haven't started working part time. Look my angel, in our country till the time parents are alive, kids don't worry about anything. Whatever you want to spend, just tell it to your Papa or me.'

'Oh! Mamma, without a full stop you are going on. You have narrated me a complete story about kids and parents in our country, without giving me a chance to speak. This is a gift from Medhansh.'

Mamma became serious, 'So expensive!'

'Not a big deal?' He has got a job; he's getting handsome salary.'

'Sara, you are talking with your mother, and not to a child. If he has got a good job he'll become a Santa Claus and start distributing gifts and that too, so expensive. I'm asking, why has he given it to you'

'He's a good friend.'

'What do you mean by a good friend,' Mamma asked trying to read her daughter's mind.

Sara wasn't trying to hide anything from her mother but she was feeling a little hesitant, thinking that her mother would wonder how soon her little angel had grown into a young lady. No matter how smart kids get but they should never think they can befool their parents or hide anything from them. Parents are always a generation ahead to them. They have seen the world, they might have also gone through the same situation in some different form, but the gist is, they can feel the pulse of their children. Sara's mother knew, from the time when she showed her the gift that something was coming. She could realize that her daughter had grown big and had started taking some independent decisions about her life. Never in the past had she accepted any gift from any friend. Now she did so, and she considered it worth showing to her mother, told her everything.

'We are serious about each other,' Sara remarked, shrinking away shyly.

'Oh, that's why he had gone to Hanuman temple. Papa and I was wondering why will anybody do such a strenuous act just for an acquaintance'

'No Mamma, even at that time, I was also astonished. It's just a few days back we got friendly.'

'When did he give you these gifts?'

'Last week, he came to meet me at my hostel, and we went for shopping.'

'And you didn't come home?'

'Yes; he came for a day, and then I was busy preparing for my presentations'

Sara's mother wanted to ask many more questions, being the mother of a young girl she was bound to act in that fashion. She restrained herself, so that Sara shouldn't feel too much of interference in her life and as a result starts hiding things from her.

'Sara, I know you are an intelligent girl. Ours is a status family. We'll never like people to raise eyebrows on our daughter for her trivial affairs; if it's something serious and you have pondered over it, we are there to support you.'

'I understand Mamma and I'm confident about it.' Sara wasn't as confident as she tried to sound in front of her mother.

Sara went back to her college, and as usual got a call from Medhansh in the evening. She shared with him, her discussion with Mamma. Sara also confided in him the apprehensions raised by her mother. Medhansh was happy to know that Sara had told her mother about their relationship, so at least, this time, he would be a winner.

'There'll be no problem. Please tell it to Mamma, I'll take care of everything,' Medhansh sounded over confident.

Sara was a bit surprised by the pace at which Medhansh was forming the relations. By now, she was also not fully sure whether she wanted to enter into a relationship with him or not, and he had already started calling her mother, Mamma. She didn't remark but thought deep down that he was a bit rustic.

On his part, Medhansh was thinking of breaking this news to his Mummy. The next moment, he got afraid as he knew his mother would be furious to know that he was preparing for his marriage, when he had an elder sister sitting unwed at home. His mother would have considered it as an offence. This was the part of family culture; ideally, he should have shared with Sara, which he thought should be better avoided if he wanted to succeed this time.

But then, it stuck to him that he would casually introduce her name to his mother; he would also promise her approval for the alliance at the right time

❧   ❧   ❧

Sara's college was celebrating the 'Rose day'. She preferred to stay in her room instead of attending the fate. Sara heard someone knocking at the door,

'Please come in.'

'Hi! Sara'

'Hi Nicky'; You are a lucky girl-countless red roses in your hand. What else you want?' Nicky knew Sara was joking as she always ridiculed girl's desperation of getting pampered by boys. She knew it was the least desired thing for Sara.

'Go downstairs; someone is anxious to meet you,' Nicky informed Sara. For a moment Sara thought, "It's Medhansh; he would have come to surprise me, or God knows shock me by another cheesy act of his."

'Who's it?'

'Go and see it for yourself.' When Sara reached the lobby she couldn't find Medhansh, and she assumed it was a prank that Nicky had played with her. She turned back and then someone called her from behind.

'Hi Sara,' she turned her head to find, it was Prateek with a red rose in his hand. She wanted to stop him there to avoid embarrassment...

'Hi Prateek, how are you?'

'Not so bad.' Prateek said presenting a rose to Sara.

'Happy Rose day'

'Thank you and same to you but I can't accept this rose from you.'

'What's wrong in it?' Prateek questioned getting prepared for any reply from Sara. Everyone knew Sara was a straight forward and overly professional girl.

'There's nothing wrong except the color. It should have been yellow.'

'How absurd, I wanted to give you a red.'

'I'm also finding it strange that without knowing my status, you are presenting me a red rose,' Sara said with a big smile on her face; she was calm and composed which was unlike her usual self.

Prateek got a little morose, 'Are you engaged?'

'Sought of, but please keep it to yourself. I don't want to publicize it.'

'Sara, you'll always be different from others. Sorry, bad luck! I didn't meet you earlier.'

Sara gave him a slight hug,' It's all destined.'

'Anyways, enjoy your day,' Prateek left the lobby but Sara could see the disappointment on his face. Sara didn't like the whole episode. Prateek didn't disturb her, but at times, she was upset with the God's sick sense of humor.

Sara was becoming emotionally dependent on Medhansh. At once, she called him, and told him about Prateek; till the time she didn't hear it from him that she handled the situation with elegance, and at times in life we are left with no options, she was feeling fidgety. After talking to him she felt placated of all her guilt's. Medhansh loved this state of Sara.

Medhansh told her that he was coming to Delhi for some official work, and would meet her in the evening for few hours. Sara was happy and started looking forward to his visit.

It was Monday; Medhansh came to her around, 4:00 p.m. They spent sometime in the nearby restaurant, and then he asked Sara to help him buy a sari for his mother. Medhansh was very fond of paper silk so he bought the same stuff cream colored sari with red motifs on it. It was a sober sari. Sara was applauding Medhansh's taste and started creating a dignified image about his mother.

Medhansh called his mother from there, 'Namaste Mummy'.

'Medhansh, where are you calling from?'

'I'm here in Delhi, and would be flying back to Hyderabad today itself.'

'Why haven't you come home?'

'I didn't have time to come. I'm here for official work, and tomorrow I have to attend a meeting in the office. I was free for some time, so I came here to meet my friend, Sara.'

'Your friend, Sara, I have never heard her name. Medhansh, you are a naive guy and these girls nowadays are crooks. Whenever they see any simple, well settled guy, they lay a trap. Beware of this Sara, Vara, whatever you named her.'

Medhansh raised his decibels over phone so that Sara also hears this part of the conversation, 'Yes Mummy, she's a very nice and simple girl. In fact, she wanted to purchase a sari to gift you, and that's what we are doing right now. There's lot of noise here, I'll call you later. Ok, bye.'

'Why did you tell your mother that I was buying her a sari, why would I? I haven't even met her,' Sara sounded upset.

'I was just making her happy as I'm unable to visit her.'

'Does that mean you would start lying; moreover, please help me understand what kind of person your mother is-she would feel happy if I gift her sari.'

Very soon Medhansh realized it was getting too chaotic, 'Ok, I'm sorry. Next time whenever I meet her, I'll tell her the truth.'

'Excuse me; this also reminds me of the statement you were giving to her, I'm a nice and simple girl. Doesn't she know about me? The day when you were forcing me to accept a gift, you told me your mother asked you to buy it for me. If she doesn't have an idea about me, then how did she ask you to do it? This is so baffling.'

'No, she knows everything about you, and how much I love you. It's just, she has a very good opinion about me, so she was telling me that if I love someone then she must be a very nice and simple girl. I don't understand why you are so negative about everything?'

Sara heard him but inwardly she wasn't feeling good about Medhansh. 'I'm from a simple educated family. We are straight forward and honest people; appreciate, if others are same with us.'

You shouldn't be concerned about my family; I promise, I would always lay it on the line.' Look at the irony of life, Medhansh was promising sincerity in future and he wasn't even being sincere at the time. He was not a charlatan, but manipulating things for someone's happiness was a harmless act for him. Sara could realize this part of his personality and several times tried telling him that this was a basic difference between them, but Medhansh always denied it with conviction; he said that God has made them for each other. He was so confident every time, that Sara would end up questioning her mentality at the end.

Things would come and go, and they would be same after that.

Sara got through an MNC bank for her summer training. She was serious about it and on completion of her college wanted to be employed there. But before that it was examination time and it was her top priority. There was no question of meeting Medhansh during those days; she was hardly talking to him over phone.

Medhansh was busy in his hectic schedule. Company was sending him to the U.S. on training for three months.

Exams were going on well and as they were coming to completion, she was excited to meet Medhansh once before he leaves for the U.S. The day arrived when Medhansh came to meet her. Sara had got attached to Medhansh. She missed him all these days. It was Medhansh who told her not to even talk over phone during exams. Despite all differences, one of the reason why Sara was attracted to Medhansh was due to his caring nature.

CHAPTER 10

'*H*I MEDHANSH, YOU DON'T know how much I missed you.'

'Good to hear these words from you! I have been always telling you about my feelings, but you are always mum. At least, today I know you love me.'

Sara felt, might be he was right, so she decided to shrug off the comment from Medhansh with a smile. It was thrilling for Medhansh, finally, he had made it and no sooner than he realized it, an idea of proposing her a honeymoon trip came to his mind. He controlled himself at that moment and thought of waiting for an opportune time.

'Sara, this time I'm here with you for complete two days and you are not going back home till the time I'm here.'

'Ok, should I get a guest room booked for you?'

'No, no!' Medhansh was irked.

'You might not get a booking afterwards.'

'You don't worry; I'll stay in some hotel.'

'Fine, you are earning now, you can very well afford it.' They moved out of Sara's hostel to start their journey. After the breakfast, they watched a movie, *Hum Tumhare Hain Sanam*; it was the best choice they had in matinee show. As usual, they came out of the movie hall arguing, both had conflicting viewpoints.

'I can't believe it, they can make such a crap! How can anyone doubt his childhood love, and be so cruel to her? This isn't love,' Sara said it emphatically, as if she was some authority on defining and assessing love.

'Sara, you should come out of your fairy tales. Love comes along with some dangerous instincts and one of them is possessiveness.'

'Oh! And what are the others?'

'Insecurity, pride etc..........'

'How funny, your package stinks!'

'This is not a package but all the emotions are interrelated.

'Ok! We can agree to disagree. Let's stop this discussion here; otherwise, it can turn you crazy,' Medhansh suggested, as he knew Sara got very serious about these emotional discussions and he wanted her to be happy for these days.

Sara knew he was right so she was also not keen to argue any further.

'Let's first go and shop for your birthday, and then we'll have lunch,' Sara seemed exhilarated

'Shopping is not required; Anyways, I'm going to U.S. I'll shop from there.'

'But I need to buy you a gift for your birthday and that's period.'

'As you say ma'am,' Sara might not have acknowledged it but she liked, *Yes ma,'am*, kind of men.

She bought him a blue grey colored blazer. 'You are looking debonair.'

Medhansh looked smart in everything he wore; he was tall, fair and handsome. He didn't require any effort to look good, he was stunning. This one factor, made him very popular among girls. Sara didn't even realize it, but initially, she was also attracted towards him due to his looks.

By that time, they were starving; they couldn't have waited more to attack a restaurant. Sara ordered pasta and Medhansh preferred his desi stuff-cottage cheese and yellow dal.

While they were waiting for the food, they saw a newlywed couple entering the restaurant. In fact, they caught everyone's attention. The boy was cuddling the girl, and she couldn't resist herself from glaring at the man even while they were walking. As soon as they sat on the table, the girl kissed him.

'Sh..........., shameless! What a showoff of love! Can't they wait to get back home and then get personal,' Sara remarked considering their behavior as an offence.

'So, you agree this behavior is love,' Medhansh asked trying to entrap her. But Sara was also smart in her thinking.

'I haven't said it, but this is what they are trying to show off. I have never denied that love generates a physical attraction but every physical attraction or intimacy is love might not be true.'

'Agreed, but you believe that love generates a physical attraction,' Medhansh was in no mood to discuss whether vice versa is true or not, it didn't serve his purpose at that time.

'Yes.'

'What about me? I love you so much. It's not a crime, why do you want to deny certain natural feelings?'

'Medhansh, at least, they are married. Can't you see those red bangles in her arms?'

'Sara, it's a question of mindset. Because you are coming from a traditional background you think so. If you wear those red bangles now, you mean to say you can justify physical relations between us. Are you bothered about this world or your feelings?'

'Of course, my feelings; you said I think so because I'm coming from a traditional background. What about your background?'

'Traditional, but I have my individuality,' Medhansh was stepping on Sara's ego by challenging her individuality.

'Oh food is here, let's finish it fast and then let's plan our two days ahead,' Medhansh wanted to give Sara a break. He could make out from her face she was getting double minded and was feeling a little tense.

After having finished the lunch, Medhansh said, 'Sara, I want to spend these two days completely with you. Please agree to it; let's go to some nearby resort. If you feel marriage is the only constraint that's stopping you, then let's go and get married now'

'Outlandish! How can you be so illusionary?'

'No, it's a good idea. I don't know when would you agree to marry me for this society, but for our conscious we can do it now. After that, I'm not bothered about this world. I can wait for the whole life. Whenever you feel like, we can get married for our families and for this society.'

Sara had started moving with the flow. She was seeing honesty and passion in Medhansh, which she herself wanted to feel for someone. She was attached to him; but still, she wasn't passionate about him.

'Ok, let's get married. I'm also not worried about this world but for my conscious these rituals are important. There should be no second thoughts after this.'

'You still think there's any scope of second thoughts?'

'I'm not saying it for myself. I told you, I have given you a commitment to be your life partner and for me things happen once in a lifetime. I'm worried about you'

'You are the only girl who wanted to be my life partner. I know you are also my first love too, there's no question of thinking twice'

They found a nearby temple and asked pujariji (priest) to perform the ceremony in brief. He did as told; they exchanged the garlands and pujariji solemnized the marriage.

'So you are happy now, we are husband and wife in the eyes of God. Let's plan our honeymoon now,' Medhansh said teasing Sara

'At times, I think you are a wicked bastard'

'Sorry ma'am, you don't have a choice now.'

Sara with dwindling mind said *yes* to Medhansh for a two days outdoor trip or in Medhansh's eyes, two days honeymoon to Manali. This was Sara's first experience of travelling alone with a boy. She knew she was putting her life, her parent's faith and reputation at stake but faith in Medhansh was compelling her to do whatever he was suggesting.

Sara wanted to pick up her luggage from the hostel, but Medhansh suggested her to do some shopping from a nearby market, rather than going back. Medhansh was skeptical if she would change her mind, once she went back to her environment. Sara agreed to buy some stuff from there and when the shopping was done, they started their journey on a deluxe bus.

Sara wasn't very comfortable in the beginning, but then after some time she started enjoying Medhansh's company. The way he was treating her with care; he was being very protective about her and Sara liked it. It was a night journey so nothing was visible outside. For a while, they were busy among themselves, discussing Medhansh's US trip, Sara's training plans and their future. They got tired after few hours and fell asleep. Medhansh woke up in between to find Sara uncomfortable in her chair. Her neck was dropping out of the chair and in her sleep she was trying to pull it back. Medhansh rotated her towards his side and ensconced her head on his shoulder. He was awake the whole night while Sara had a nice sleep. She opened her eyes with the first beam of sun and got stunned to see the scenic beauty outside. They were moving down into a valley with mountains on one side and on the other side, it was a dancing river under the clean blue sky, electrified to meet its guest and wanted to accompany them to their destination.

They reached Manali and a fresh journey of life started for Sara. It was a new experience, first time she was feeling a man so closely. It was her age or unrealized love for Medhansh, she was enjoying every moment with him but with some heaviness on mind. She wasn't at ease with the thought that her parents were unaware of what she was doing.

Two days fled away and they reached back to Sara's hostel. It was time to say good-bye for a bit longer duration. Both were feeling melancholy and didn't wish to part away; however, life has to move on, and with a tight hug and a kiss, they parted their ways.

Next day, Sara came back to her home for summer vacation and training. When Diya saw her, she said, 'Sara you are looking gorgeous today; it seems you are in love.' Sara was surprised to hear this from her little sister; she thought, "Has Diya grown old so soon or is her face looking so prominent?"

'Diya has grown big; let me ask Mamma to get you married.'

'I have already asked them.'

'Where's the guy?'

'Sara, he was always in front of your eyes but you have never noticed him. My dear sister, it's not that I have grown big; you are still small, Mamma's baby.'

Sara wanted to tell her that she was no more a baby; she had gone too far away from Mamma.

'Stop this nonsense! You, tell me who's the guy'

'Of course, Ankit.'

'That enthusiastic kiddo'

'Sara, at least, treat him with some dignity,' and the sisters laughed.

Diya told Sara that both of them were planning to go to U.S. for their higher studies, and they wanted to apply in different universities as a couple, which meant before the completion of their engineering they wanted to be married.

Sara's mother came back rushing from her clinic, as soon as she got a call from Sara.

'Oh my sweet heart, you are back,' Mamma hugged her.

'How are you Mamma? Don't worry, I'm here with you for more than a month'

Meanwhile, Sara's father also came in. Sara ran towards him and cuddled him like a kid.

'My little princess, how much I missed you?' Everyone in the family was delighted.

'Mamma, has Diya told you something about her future plans'

'That's the first thing she's telling to everyone nowadays. I don't know when she would grow up. My all hopes are on Ankit now. I feel he will be matured enough to handle her.'

'Then, you are going to be proved wrong. He's such a sweet kid, I don't think he'll ever get a chance to handle Diya, she'll be managing him all the time'

'Don't scare me Sara.'

'Ok, you wait and watch.'

Sara's father interrupted in between, I need to talk to Sara first. Sara, do you find Ankit suitable for Diya?'

'Papa, Ankit is a very nice, respectful guy; but more important is what Diya thinks about him. If she is making this choice based on professional compatibility then I think she must re consider her decision, but if she feels for him from core of her heart and loves him for a person he is, then she can never be wrong. Our all blessings should be with her.'

'I can never think of anyone else except Ankit in my life,' Diya said with a hoarse voice.

Mamma kept a hand on her head and kissed her, 'We all like Ankit; Our best wishes are with you.'

'Just one more thing, I wanted to ask Sara about her future plans. Diya is younger to you; we will like you to get married before her,' Papa said

'Papa, these are age old thoughts. If she has found her life partner let her go her own way. I'm not yet prepared for marriage. I'll like to focus on my career'

'Dear, don't pass a statement in haste; yours is the right age for marriage, think about it and if you don't want to discuss it with me, talk to your Mamma about it.'

'Ok, can we give it a break and have dinner. I'm sure we are going to have the same discussions for the complete coming month, so keep some stock for future,' Mamma said.

She was startled by Sara's reaction. She thought, "Sara was serious about Medhansh, then why did she tell her father that she wasn't prepared for marriage."

After dinner, when Sara was sitting alone with her mother in the living room, Mamma asked, 'How's Medhansh?'

'He's Fine.'

'When did you last meet him?'

Sara got a little scared that her mother might not dig deep into it, but she decided to answer her everything honestly, 'this weekend.'

'That's why you didn't come on the weekend.'

'He is going to US for three months and wanted to meet me before leaving.'

'Is everything ok between two of you?'

'Yes, we are good friends,' Sara couldn't understand the reason of hiding her relationship from her mother when she knew Mamma could feel everything.

'Sara, I feel, your mind is still not fixed about him. You should be clear about your emotions. Anyways, I would also like to meet him whenever he's back; for the first time my daughter has called some guy a friend.'

134

'Mamma you have met him so many times. What's new in him?'

'Earlier I used to meet him as a Diya's senior, now I would like to see my daughter's friend.'

'Fine, I'll pass on the message, whenever he's back.'

'Good night Angel; it's too late, you must be tired'

'Good night Mamma,' Sara was happy to come back to her room as she wanted to escape her queries. Sara was relaxed to find her mother being aware of their relationship. She was also mentally prepared for the next level of questions by her, any which day.

She slept well that night; she knew, she had a few leisure days to enjoy at home and after that she would be busy with her summer training. She was enjoying her lethargic routine at home. Once, Ankit came home and three of them went out for dinner; apart from that she was at home; eating and sleeping.

She joined her training. Sara was impressed with the plush office, and king size room of her reporting boss, Abhimanyu. Abhimanyu was an MBA Finance from abroad and was heading the treasury division of the bank. He was a handsome and an intelligent guy who was known for his result orientation. No cheese on his face, he was a stern looking guy and a man of few words.

Sara entered his room, 'Good morning, Sir'

Abhimanyu raised his brows, and his looks gave shivers to Sara, 'Call me Abhimanyu'

'Abhimanyu, I'm Sara from FMS and I would be doing my summer project under your guidance'

'I have your complete details in front of me, so take it easy. Take this folder, I have assigned you a project and some references are also attached. Take a day to go through them, and submit a draft project plan by tomorrow. Bye; see you.'

Sara found it too rude and arrogant. But sometimes these ragging sessions at colleges are of real help to you in your practical life. In the college, first thing, she learnt was, 'Seniors are always right.' It was time to implement it.

'Bye, Abhimanyu.' When she opened her file, she could see a project on *Hedging Strategies*. It was something of Sara's liking. At last, she felt positive about Abhimanyu.

His PA (Personal Assistant) was sitting in a bay outside his room and as soon as she saw Sara coming out of the door, she stood up to greet her.

'Hi I'm Nancy; I'll show you the bay. You can fill the requisition form for the stationery, and I'll issue the items. Abhimanyu is a very meticulous guy and he likes perfection.'

'I can see it in the manner things are arranged here,' Sara said, not knowing whether to sound sarcastic or appreciative of him. She was feeling as if she had entered the world of Robots; whereas, she was expecting a cordial environment. Within an hour of being seated there, she realized the environment was very warm and friendly; only Abhimanyu was an alien. Leaving all this behind, she started studying her project with full concentration. There was tremendous work to be done in a short span of time.

By 6:00 p.m., most of the office staff had left and even Nancy had also left for the day. Sara didn't know whom to report to before leaving. She could see Abhimanyu busy in a meeting. She waited for him to get free. She sat in her bay studying her papers. It was 8:00 p.m., when he came out of the meeting. Sara rushed to his room.

'Excuse me, Abhimanyu'
'You are still here!'
'You were in a meeting....'
'So!'

'I thought I should inform you before going.'

'Did someone tell you that you have to report before leaving? Sara, this is a corporate world and you have to be crisp in whatever you do.

'Sorry, I'll be careful.' Sara thought, "What an idiot he is? Instead of appreciating my sincerity and showing concern about me, as it is so late, he is lecturing me. He just seems to be a money minting machine. How unlucky his wife would be?"

Sara rushed to the parking, unlocked her car and drove rashly to reach home at the earliest. She was tense when she got back. Her mother asked her the reason and she narrated about the whole day, 'What a stressful man he is?'

Her mother laughed, 'No, he's just training you to be a professional; you kids are too much in your comfort zone.'

'How can you support him Mamma? He's a mad man.'

Sara was up till late, working on her project plan and the next morning, she was gratified at her achievement. Life started moving up- and- down. It was very difficult to impress Abhimanyu. He was always demanding. However good Sara felt she had done, Abhimanyu eye for details would always find some gaps, and Sara felt demoralized. It wasn't that he always criticized her for her work, in between he also appreciated her for good going but it used to be one of a day. Sara started taking it in a stride, and was least bothered about his reaction. She was happy that she was learning a lot with him.

Saturday morning; while she was still in bed, Sara could hear the phone ringing in living room and she waited for someone to pick it up.

'Hello, Dr Sanial here.'

'Hi Sidhant, could I speak to Sara?'

'Sara, phone for you from Sidhant'

Sara jumped out of her bed, completely baffled. "I know only one Sidhant, but why has he called me?" Sara's mother handed over the cradle to her and moved away. Sara could barely speak

'Hi, Sidhant.'

'Hello Sara,' Sara could hear the same bold, confident voice.

'How are you? After a long time,' Sara was falling short of words; her heart was throbbing.

'I was just settling down in the U.S.'

'How are you finding the U.S.?'

'There's nothing great. Every place is same. It depends on you, how you take it,' he was the same person, so casual; couldn't answer anything straight. Only thing exceptional was, he was saying too many words to Sara.

'Oh! Good.'

'How is your new college?'

'Nothing great, very ordinary like every other college,' Sara realized that she was talking in his parlance, so she immediately changed her tone; 'I like it, and now a day's I'm doing my summer training.'

'How do you spend your day?' Sidhant asked, as if he was least interested to hear about her college and her training and wanted to know more about her.

'I'm busy in office the whole day; after that, there's nothing much to be done'

Pause...............

'So, you haven't changed a bit; still workaholic'

'No, I just do whatever is required to be done,' Sara was inanimate, unable to say anything.

Sidhant realized that she was not herself due to some reason, 'Sara, are you ok? You seem to be a little disturbed.'

'I'm perfectly fine. I was sleeping when you called up so maybe I'm sounding low'

'I'm sorry if I have disturbed you.'

'Please don't say it, good you called ....'

'Sara, I'll have to hang up the phone; there's someone at the door. I'll call you later.

'Okay bye'

'Bye, stay in touch,' Sara couldn't understand the reason of her last sentence; it just flowed out of her mouth.

It became a *stressful saturday* for her. She wanted to relax on the weekend, but Sidhant's phone had confused her so much, that all her anxiety about him was back. She was getting a bad taste in her mouth; when she thought about Sidhant, and memories of her relationship with Medhansh were flashing before her eyes.

When she reached back office on Monday, it was for the first time, Abhimanyu looked at her and said, 'You look tired, what happened?'

'I'm fine Abhimanyu, thanks'

'It's okay, if you don't want to share; fact is you are looking too exhausted after a weekend'

'It's a little personal.'

'I'm sorry,' Abhimanyu straight away jumped on the project discussion. Sara was almost on the completion stage of her project, and was to submit her project report within a week. Nowadays he was discussing the draft with Abhimanyu. The day was going normal. It was just she preferred to be quiet and alone. The more she wanted to lead a straight forward and confusion free life, the lesser she would get of it. She was settling down with Medhansh, and Sidhant was again back in her life. She wanted to talk to Medhansh about it and desperately needed his shoulders to cry on. The idea of sharing it with him over phone, and disturbing him, when he was too far away didn't appeal her. She decided to overcome her anxiety on her own.

It was getting difficult for her to concentrate on the office work. Abhimanyu was in a meeting, so she informed Nancy and called it a day. When Abhimanyu came out of the meeting, he asked for Sara, as he wanted to give some feedback about her report. Nancy told him that she had gone back, he couldn't desist himself from expressing his unhappiness over her gesture, 'She should have met me before leaving.'

'She looked for you but you were in a meeting, so she left the message with me,' Nancy said defending Sara.

'Anyways, she should have told me if she wanted to leave early.'

Nancy wanted to tell him that he himself never liked the idea of anyone waiting for him; however, she couldn't have dared to say it to him.

Sara reached back home and opted to sleep. In the evening, she wanted a much needed break so she asked Diya to come along with her for a long drive. They also invited Ankit for a dinner after the drive. It was a good change for Sara. Her mind was diverted for a while and she felt relaxed.

The next day, she reached office to find Abhimanyu a little upset. He didn't tell her anything directly but his facial expressions said everything. They exchanged few papers without saying much and she came out of his room.

'Nancy, Is he disturbed today?'

'It's not because of today, but yesterday. He was looking for you after you had left and he was upset to know that you had gone without meeting him. Never mind, you know how he is!'

'A funny guy'

'No, an extremely funny..............., Nancy giggled.

Abhimanyu was okay in the evening, report was almost finalized. He was happy with the outcome. He also complimented Sara for all the hard work and seriousness shown by her during training. Sara took it with a smile and thanked him for his kind words. Only three days were left for her training and she was in a winding up mode. Her presentation was planned for the second last day.

Sara came well prepared on the day of presentation. She sounded confident and knowledgeable. Everyone present there admired Sara for her efforts and congratulated Abhimanyu for being a good leader he was. Abhimanyu was enthused with pride, first time a broad smile was visible on his face. After the presentation Sara approached Abhimanyu, 'Thanks Abhimanyu, for all the guidance and support'

'I didn't do you a favor, it was my job,' Abhimanyu was as rude as he always was.

'Sara, what are you doing tomorrow?'

'Nothing much, I would be spending some time with friends here.'

'Why don't you join me for lunch?'

Sara was thrilled as it would be her first corporate lunch and moreover, she was also impressed by Abhimanyu for his professional capabilities, 'Sure, why not?'

'"12 o'clock", we we'll go from here.'

'Okay.'

Sara was trying to come out of Sidhant's phone. She got a chance to further distract her mind. She started planning on what she would wear for the next day.

It was Friday; she decided to wear the denim jeans with a white shirt. Sara looked charismatic in whites.

The Last day; to show her gratitude Sara bought some souvenirs for people like Nancy with whom she got close.

'Hi Nancy, so I won't be troubling you after today.'

'Don't say like that dear, we would all miss you a lot, but I'm happy for you.'

'What's so special?'

'At least, you'll be free from the torture; you won't have to tolerate him anymore.'

'Who? Abhimanyu! He's a sweet guy'

'Is everything okay with you?'

'I'm going out on a lunch with him'

'What????' Nancy dropped the pen in her hand and her mouth was wide open.

'It looks so cheap, shut your mouth.'

'Are you sure, you are having lunch with Abhimanyu?'

'Nancy, how can I say no to him, besides I'm going out on my first corporate lunch.'

'Best of luck sweety, I hope everything goes well and you don't step on his fragile ego anytime'

'I'll take care of it, thanks for making me conscious'

12 o'clock: Abhimanyu came out of his room and straight away moved towards elevator. Sara had to make an effort to keep pace with him. He had to stop for the lift; otherwise, he was running a marathon. Meanwhile Sara reached there, 'Hi'. He just smiled and turned his face straight towards the elevator. Sara wondered if he had done some favor by inviting her, his behavior irked her. On spur of a moment Abhimanyu turned his face again towards her and first time gave her an appreciative look. Sara felt a little better. He drove her to Taj Mansingh, a five star hotel in Delhi. He started walking inside and Sara tried following him. It was very suffocating for Sara. It was a one sided affair and Abhimanyu was the person driving it. She was apprehensive, if he would even ask her about her preference of food.

'What kind of food would you like to have?'

"Thanks God!"

'White, white pasta.'

They entered the lobby and he straight away started walking to a restaurant, *Machan*, on that level.

He ordered a clear vegetable soup and grilled sandwich for himself and mushroom sauced pasta for Sara.

'Sara, I'm a blunt person and without mincing any words I would like to come to the point. 'It shocked Sara to realize that they had gone there with a purpose.

'My parents are old and they want me to get married. I have ignored their demand for a long.'

Sara couldn't control herself, 'Are you a bachelor?'

'What do you mean? Are you suggesting me that I'm too old to be a bachelor?'

'No I can never mean that, I want to say that how can a guy like you, so handsome, intelligent and successful be still a bachelor in this country.' Sara was trying to save her skin, and she was paying a penalty for being kiddish.

'Sorry, you were saying something.'

'I would appreciate if you let me complete,' Abhimanyu sounded displeased.

'Please go ahead............'

'My parents want me to get married and it seems, with you I can work out a deal. You are intellectual, but at times babyish, which should improve with time.'

Sara wanted to, "slap him or splash on him a glass of water lying on the table. She wanted to tell him, she hadn't come across an idiot like him and she would prefer to end her life rather than doing something as dreadful as marrying him."

Sara controlled herself, 'Abhimanyu, you are a dream guy for any girl but I'm so unfortunate, I can't say you, *yes*. I'm already engaged, but I'm honored you considered me worth you. I'm sorry.............'

'Never mind, I wasn't very serious, but thought this can be explored. Let's finish our lunch. I need to rush for a meeting.'

White pasta seemed black pasta to Sara, she was feeling nauseatic. She couldn't eat anything. On his side, Abhimanyu felt offended by Sara, and as it was visible from his face but he tried ignoring it.

'Let's move and they reached back to the office. Abhimanyu rushed back to his cabin and Sara to her bay. Nancy saw Sara and without delay came rushing towards her,

'How was the lunch? Do you need some sandwiches?'

'Yes, I'm feeling very hungry, anything will do.'

'I knew this is going to happen. His parents are desperate to find a girl for him. I'm sure she'll commit suicide in a day'

Sara smirked, 'Even I think so.' She grabbed a sandwich from Nancy; ordered a black coffee, and sat in the cafeteria, to find some relief after the torturous incident. But Sara was thinking that it won't be easy for her to survive in this world with a "single" status. Every other man would find her approachable and in this way she might not be able to exist anywhere. She made up her mind to think about an early marriage and whenever her father next talks about it, she would yield. She was absolutely clear that her dream of joining that bank had gone for a toss. Abhimanyu would never let it happen.

For good, it was time to say bye to everyone; she went to Abhimanyu's room and said good-bye to him. Outside it was an emotional scene, all friends and colleagues were there with bouquets and gifts. They all walked Sara to her car.

While Sara was driving back home, she wanted to stop the car in between and laugh. Abhimanyu talking to her something that ridiculous was the least desired, or thought off thing for her.

Sara was at home for a few more days. While she was going back to hostel, Mamma reminded her to ask Medhansh to meet her whenever he was back from US.

CHAPTER 11

*S*ARA SUBMITTED THE PROJECT report in the college and made the presentation. The concerned faculty applauded Sara for the commendable work she had done.

She again became busy with her lectures, case studies and extra curricula's.

After a few days Medhansh came back from the U.S. As soon as he reached the airport he called up Sara to inform her that he was coming to meet her. Sara was in high spirits.

Before he could say anything, Sara had a long story to tell him. She told him about her training, Abhimanyu and how he tried making a deal with her.

Medhansh wasn't so happy to hear it,' Sara finish your studies and let's get married.'

'Even, I thought about it. By the way, Mamma wanted to meet you.'

'Did you tell her about us?'

'Not everything, but she has some clue.'

'Ok, I'll meet her after Nina's marriage.'

'Is she getting married? You never told me about it.'

'I wasn't even aware of it. Mohit called me up a few days back to inform me about it.'

'How did it happen?'

'She liked a guy in her college and now his family has approached us. They are a wealthy business family, so Mummy is interested in the alliance.'

'Congrats! It's good your sister will be marrying her love.'

'Thanks, I hope everything goes well. This time I'm not going home as I need to be in Hyderabad today itself. Next week I'll go there so won't be able to meet you; it might be the case for next few weeks, till the time marriage is over.'

'Okay.'

The Next week, Medhansh reached home. He was curious to meet the guy but his mother was anxious to gauge his financial contribution in the marriage. Her mother gave him an estimate of forty lakhs to be spent on the marriage, and told him at the max they would be able to arrange fifteen lakhs and rest twenty five lakhs needed to come from him. Not even once he asked about the reason to have such an expensive wedding, if it wasn't within their reach. Since childhood, Medhansh's mother had groomed him to be an obedient son who would take care of the whole family. He was good at studies from the very beginning, whereas his brother had always been good-for-nothing, so Medhansh's mother had stuffed in his mind that he was the only hope of the family. However, Medhansh never considered it worthwhile to share it with Sara, the expectations his family had from him. He always considered it to be there internal family affair and Sara by no means would have to do anything with it. He loved Sara because of her non-interfering and self- reliant nature.

Nina's, marriage was solemnized. Everything was quintessential, as per Mummy's satisfaction and everyone appreciated the lavish arrangements done. For Medhansh, it was the mission accomplished of making his mother happy.

'Hi, are you still at home or back to Hyderabad,' Sara called up Medhansh.

'I would be flying tomorrow'

'How was the marriage?'

'Good; anyways, who cares? Mohit and Mummy were there to take care of everything. These are family formalities; you just need to be a part of it, nothing more,' Medhansh invariably tried to project his indifference towards his family. Sara every time got an impression that he wanted to be freed from that environment.

'Sara, one interesting incident happened. Daddy asked me to meet his friend's daughter. At the beginning, I said, "No," but then I realized I have upset him. I decided to go and meet Manya. I also took Tina along with me so that it wasn't too embarrassing for me. Manya was beautiful but clumsy. I can't believe! She ordered potato wedges as starters, isn't it too desi. When I came back home, I told Mummy to handle Daddy in future. I have also asked her to tell him about our relationship.'

'Medhansh, I'm finding you clumsy and not Manya. In this progressive age, if a twenty five year old guy can't talk straight to his Daddy about his relationship, then no one can be a bigger desi than him. Moreover, you should have been descent enough not to play with the emotions of a girl, what if Manya had liked you?'

'Sara, I was sure I would reject her, and I also ensured it by behaving gauche that she doesn't like me.'

'Medhansh, at times, I find you too self centered and a meek personality. You think things can be designed by you in life, to work in a way you want. You should have been bold and open in front of your Daddy, rather than putting it on your Mummy.'

'Sara, I have always been submissive. I want to change myself and the reason I like you so much is because you have the strength which can help me transform.'

Medhansh didn't sound convincing to Sara. She never wanted anyone to change for her. She always believed in one's real self, but if Medhansh didn't change as per his promise, it would mean a lot of cultural and personality differences between them. She didn't have any choice, but to have faith in him.

'Why are you quiet? I'll handle everything. I'm so close to you after three months, look at the irony, again over the phone; at least, give me a kiss,' and as usual he diverted Sara from the heavy discussion.

'Medhansh, now I have a cell phone xxxxxxxxxx. Call me on this number if anything urgent .Still I'm not earning so I'm using it for a limited purpose'

'Your parents have enough money to give it to you'

'No, I want to be self dependent'

'Just joking; Ok, bye'

⟜ ⟜ ⟜

Unexpectedly, Sara received a call from Avni the next day.

'Guess, who's on the line?'

'Hi Avni, after a long time! How are you?' Sara didn't even take a second to recognize her voice.

'I'm in high spirits, what about you?'

'Not bad. How's your PG (Post Graduation) going on?' Sara said avoiding any discussion about her.

'You'll always remain a book worm. Your college friend of marriageable is calling you after a year and you are asking her about her PG. Sara, you are the only one who can do it. If I see you beyond books," at times", "no always", I find you dumb.'

'Fine ma'am, so you are getting married'

'Yes...............'

'Who's the guy?'

'Once more you are raising a concern on your IQ. Of course, it has to be Jimmy.'

'Congrats! I'm happy for both of you but with my limited IQ, let me tell, both of you need to hold tight each other throughout life; otherwise you two are so light that any breeze can take you away anytime.

'Funny! Are you being sarcastic or trying to hint at something.'

'Avni, my friend, I'm trying to tell that you two are so sweet that you need to be watchful of each other. This institution gives you an attitude of taking each other for granted. Never get into that mode.'

'You are sounding too philosophical. Are you involved with someone?'

'I would never commit such a blunder,' Sara avoided telling the fact to Avni; she never realized that Avni was seeking this information to pass onto someone.

'Anyways, next month we are getting married and you are coming to my place for at least, a week.'

'Not to say, I'll be there.'

Sara went with her Mamma to buy wedding gifts for Avni and Jimmy. She bought a south silk sari for Avni from Nali's and a shirt for Jimmy. She also called up Medhansh to tell him about Avni's marriage and that she had planned to attend it. Medhansh wasn't very comfortable on her going alone there but then Sara expressed her helplessness to take him along with her.

Sara went to attend Avni's marriage. She enjoyed every ceremony. It was an elaborate and lavish affair. The lehnga Avni wore on her wedding day costed around two lakh. She looked gorgeous, and a responsible girl; very different from that mini skirt kind. When she got ready, Sara gave her a hug and both of them busted into tears. At that time Sara realized, she was missing someone else and the environment was making her namby pamby.

Jimmy's family was also staying in the same hotel. Sara went to meet him in his room. She could find Rohit and many others cracking jokes with him. When Sara entered the room they all became quiet and Sara straight away moved towards Jimmy, she could still see some void in the eyes of Jimmy when he saw her. Sara could feel the pain, no one could have done anything about it, and time takes its own course to fill such passing affairs. She gave a hug to Jimmy and congratulated him. Her eyes were moving around the room looking for Sidhant, she knew he wasn't there yet her heart made her helpless.

Sara came back; instead of going back to hostel she preferred to take one more day off and went to home. She was getting emotional and required to be with her mother for some time. Her mother misunderstood her behavior to be age related and reminded her to invite Medhansh over a cup of tea.

Sara communicated the same to Medhansh and asked him to plan a visit in a week or two. Medhansh promised to accompany her next week. That week, he had planned a visit to his home. Medhansh wanted to go home with a purpose to finalize his marriage with Sara. Initial few hours were routine at home, and then when Medhansh and his Mummy were chatting over a cup of tea, his Mummy remarked,

'My scion, you forget about that girl Sara, Vara. You have taken so much of loan for your sister's marriage, we need a girl who can support you and duly compensate us. You have one more sister who is unwed.'

'Mummy, her name is Sara and I have told you, I'm marrying her'

The assertiveness in Medhansh's voice offended Mummy, 'I didn't expect this from you. I thought you'll take care of your family. You know your father was never a reliable man and your elder brother is a loafer, to top it off he has turned into a Romeo. If you are showing me your tantrums now, what's going to happen after your marriage? You are going to be no different from your brother. I'm ruined............' she started yelling and this was a common sight if someone didn't agree to her. Medhansh wanted to pacify her and meet his target.

'Mummy, you are so sharp and intelligent. Sara is an engineer, MBA and she would be always earning. She would be like a golden hen for you. Now you decide if you want one time return or a continuous flow throughout your life.'

'How would you ensure that she always does for our family?'

'She belongs to a traditional family, she would never go against her husband and I know she would be always so happy with me that I can make her do anything.'

'My innocent son, these girls are very cunning now a day's; yet if you are convinced, I have no choice but to have faith on you.' Medhansh could hit his target.

He confirmed Sara about his visit next week to her home. The next week, he went to Sara's house. Medhansh's sincerity and commitment impressed Mamma. She requested everyone that she would like to meet Medhansh in isolation.

'Medhansh, what kind of relationship you have with Sara. If it's ambiguous, I would like you to stop meeting my daughter from now on.'

'Mamma, I thought Sara would have told you.'

'No, I wanted to talk to you before asking her. She's a very emotional and innocent girl.'

'I'm not interested in having any other relationship except lifelong commitment. In case she isn't prepared for it, I can assure you, this will be our last meeting.'

'God Bless You, I'll ask her what she wants. I will like to visit your house along with Sara's father to finalize the things.'

'Anytime Mamma......'

After Medhansh had left the house, Mamma spoke to Sara about it.

'Mamma, I like him. I'm committed to him but I'm still not convinced if I want to marry him now.'

'What non sense? I thought you were sensible enough to understand how your father would react if he comes to know about your views. Sara, you are always so indecisive. Let me tell you, if you are meeting him again then you are marrying him.'

'Ok Mamma. I'm fine with it, whatever you decide,' Sara wanted to run away from this discussion without realizing how important this decision is for anyone's life.

'Concentrate on your studies for now and get yourself a job. I'll take it forward after that.'

Sara got busy with her studies and Medhansh in his job. They used to meet once in two months and everything was amicable among them. Sara was settling with the idea of marrying Medhansh. They had started discussing about shifting to one location, and many other critical aspects.

Sara's term was coming to an end. For her winter project, she got an opportunity to do it with the same bank, and for good, she got the final job offer from there. She used to meet Abhimanyu, he was always professional and the very fact that she got a job offer showed he was a man of principles. Sara's emotions swayed her at times, and she wanted to give Abhimanyu some feedback on improving his personal aspects of life. She wished to see him happy; however, the fear of getting misunderstood always restrained her.

Diya and Ankit were all set to get married. They gave their preference for a simple ceremony accompanied by a close family get together. It was a small gathering. Medhansh was an invitee on Diya's marriage and he was formally introduced as a "would be son in law". The news shocked Ankit. Diya was sitting beside him for a ring ceremony,' Diya when did it happen?'

'What?'

'Sara getting involved with Medhansh.'

'Even I wasn't aware, it was just a few days back Mamma called him home, and from what I realize they had been going together for the last three years. I thought Medhansh would have told you.'

'No one has told me anything. At least, Sara should have talked to us. What does she know about him?'

'Come on Ankit! She is not a kid. They are together for the last three years and I'm sure she will know everything about him.'

'Anyways, I need to talk to Sara once. I'm hurt; I thought we were close enough, for her to share such an important decision with me.'

'Ok, please don't spoil your mood now. Let's start our life on an auspicious note.'

Ankit regaining his calm said, 'Sure, sweet heart'.

Ankit was just waiting for the ceremony to get over and no sooner than it happened he rushed to Sara. Sara was sitting alone.

'Hi groom, how are you roaming without your bride?'

'Sara I wanted to talk to you, it's urgent!'

'Is everything ok? Is anything wrong between you and Diya?'

'No between you and me.'

They moved to a room,' Yes, tell me Ankit. I'm scared'

'Sara I thought, we were friends before anything else. You didn't find me worth to have shared with me your relationship with Medhansh.'

'I'm sorry Ankit. I wasn't sure how would you react after he told me about his affairs in the past.'

'Amazing! He told you about everything'

'Yes, and that's what I liked about him- honesty'

'He is a seasoned player. You know he's very erratic and opportunist.'

'Now I have started realizing it about him, but then no one is perfect in this world. I feel he should be given a chance to prove his sincerity. May be he was always true but girls used him for being emotional.'

'One last question, do you love him?'

'I'm too naive to understand what love is, but I'm sure we can stay together for life and he can manage me'.

Ankit realized that it was too late to explain anything to Sara but he was apprehensive about Sara's feeling. After talking to Sara he realized, she wanted to do it because he was honest and did few promises to her,' so she committed to stay with him for life without understanding what this relationship might demand in future-"love"

'Ok Sara; but never forget, whenever, you need me just call me once and I'll be there.'

'Why are you getting so emotional Ankit for your sister-in-law?'

'No, I'm concerned about my friend and for gem of a person,' Sara gave him a hug and kissed him on his forehead. When they came out Diya could see sparkles of tears in Ankit's eyes. She could do nothing but just wonder.

CHAPTER 12

*M*AMMA TOLD MEDHANSH ABOUT their plan to visit his house on the coming weekend. Medhansh panicked and rushed back home to do some preparations for the visit of Sara's parents.

When the weekend came, Sara's parents were leaving the house to go to Medhansh's place, and Sara accompanied them to the car. Mamma looked at Sara's face and she seemed nervous.

'Sara, don't get upset. We aren't going there to decide anything. You have taken a decision and we are going there just to formalize the relationship. You have our nod right now.'

Sara's parents were not the cause of worry for her. She knew they loved her and respected her choice. The problem was, she wasn't herself too convinced about her choice and additionally she had doubts about his family as Medhansh had always tried to avoid discussing them.

His family was simple, not too educated, and not like the ones who could have enthused Sara's parents. Sara's mother was a little perturbed by the visible cultural differences. His mother who seemed to be less educated, looked insecure, manipulative and like a political woman. But like most of the Punjabi women of that category, she always behaved in a sugar-coated way. His father was a suppressed man and the mother seemed to be the decision-maker of the family. Sara's mother was most disturbed by the insecurity of Medhansh's mother and dependence on Medhansh. The visit was cool and both the families parted on a harmonious note.

When Sara's parents came back home, she was anxious to know their feedback. Sara knew her father was a traditional man and would have preferred marrying her to someone from their community. Her mother expressed her honest concerns to Sara, intending not to discourage her but to make her mind prepared for the adjustments and compromises that might be, in store for her in the future.

'Mamma, I'll never have to face those differences. Medhansh has promised me to take care of everything and I'll always be his first priority.'

At times, kids make their parents so helpless that even knowing the future they have no choice but to keep quiet. Parents educate their kids and give them that wisdom of making independent decisions. When they make their decisions without the experience that age can provide, parents can only wish for the best. This was the case with Sara's parents; they knew saying anything against their daughter's first love would just make her rebellious and they never wanted to lose their daughter. They were happy in whatever she wanted for her life.

After a month, the wedding was planned, and Medhansh's parents expressed their desire to make it a grand affair. Sara disagreed with this idea, but her parents and Medhansh convinced her to let it be a traditional marriage.

Sara and Medhansh used to go shopping on weekends when he came from Hyderabad. Medhansh got himself transferred to the Delhi office so they were also hunting for a rented accommodation in Delhi. They found a flat in South Delhi and started furnishing it. Medhansh was unable to pay for any of the bills, so Sara paid it from her savings, and by that time she had also received her first salary.

'Medhansh, where's all your money gone? It's been more than two years that you have been working and you haven't saved anything for your future.'

'I have spent all my savings on my sister's marriage and to top it off, I had to take a fifteen lakhs loan which is still unpaid. Few EMI's are left.'

Sara was astonished to hear it, 'You never told me about your financial concerns and liabilities.'

'Would you have changed your decision? Please do it now. It was a family obligation and I thought this will be my last chance to do something for my family, as I'll have my responsibilities afterwards.'

Sara didn't like his brazen attitude, 'You should have, at least, shared it with me.'

'I'm sorry. I didn't think it would concern you as I was sure I would repay this loan before our marriage But then your mother got in a hurry to get us married.'

'Anyways, you should have told me about your monetary state, and regarding my mother, any mother would be concerned about her daughter's future if she's in a dwindling relationship.'

Medhansh got a little self-conscious and changed his tone. He knew Sara was capable of calling it a day whenever she got offended. 'I'll give you all my finances to handle in future.'

Money was not a concern for Sara, but his attitude of hiding things disturbed her. Medhansh was smart enough to cajole her to go for a movie and then dinner afterwards. They had a nice day, and Sara was happy with him, indulging in shopping and doing her house decor.

Finally, the big day arrived. Sara, at least, kept it a simple affair for herself. She chose to wear a red silken straight lehnga with light golden embroidery on it. She wore very light makeup and jewellery, unlike a typical Indian bride who is loaded with them. Sara looked beautiful.

Medhansh arrived with his family, very late as per the scheduled time. It's very typical of Indian families from the groom side, who consider reaching on time would demean them, so they prefer to reach late on most of the important occasions to gain importance and respect. What an irony? However, Sara's family didn't appreciate the move as they all were cultured people, and respected punctuality. But then they didn't have any choice but to welcome them with broad smiles and folded hands.

Sara came out in the venue where the marriage ceremony was to be solemnized. Since the previous night, a depression had been settling in on her. She was getting a feeling that something wrong was happening that should be stopped. She wasn't sure what made her so sulky, or with whom she could share her feelings. The evening before when she spoke to Medhansh, she told him about her thoughts. Medhansh pacified her by telling her that it was a typical case of anxiety any girl would feel before marriage.

She was walking the aisle like an angel. Her pretty lehnga was flowing on the ground, giving her a majestic look. Medhansh glanced at her with adoring eyes. She wasn't too keen to look at him. Pujari ji asked Sara to sit along with Medhansh and that was the time she had to anyways, look at him; she gave him an awkward smile and sat beside him. The rituals were to be followed by a reception party. It was difficult for Sara to behave like a typical Indian bride, so she was moving here and there taking Medhansh along with her in the party, meeting people and trying to make herself comfortable. It was a cultural shock for Medhansh's family. His mother was frowning on Sara's behavior, which she didn't find befitting a bride. Sara expected Medhansh to ignore it and focus on them; after all, it was their day. On the contrary, Medhansh was busy comforting his family. So much so, to take out his frustration he even passed a derogatory remark on her attire. Sara was hurt due to his rude behavior, and this was how they started their new life, with a friction.

It was a nice marriage for rest of the world, even for their parents.

The next day, they started for their honeymoon; mission accomplished for Medhansh. But instead of getting closer to each other, a fragile foundation of their marriage was laid down during these days. They started having arguments about Medhansh's family. One day Medhansh became so aggressive that he even commented, 'If you have any problems settling with my mother, in that case you'll have to leave the house.' It was an impossible moment for a short-tempered and egoistic Sara. She wanted to dump him and fly back; yet she tried ignoring it because she was conscious of the commitment she had made. One thing was very clear, instead of advancing her liking into love, these days were sufficient to widen the gap between them. In those five days, Medhansh seemed very casual about the relationship. He projected an attitude toward her of taking her for granted. It was too much, too soon. It seemed Medhansh was in a hurry to change his priorities. *His love was like putting a feather in his cap and he immediately wanted to move to the next milestone.* His family and career became his priorities. He was eager to go back to attend some important meeting with his director. Sara felt cheated.

Sara wasn't keen on staying there, so they came back within a week. She became busy with her job but there was stress on the work front as well. It was just three months into the job when she'd taken this break for the honeymoon. Already there's so much bias against female employees at the workplace and above it, she felt that getting married within three months of joining was tantamount to ruining her career. She started making extra efforts to prove herself.

After a few months of being married, Medhansh's daddy faced a huge loss in his business. A client rejected a very big consignment, and it wasn't completely insured.

At 10 p.m. one night, the phone buzzed. Medhansh picked it up.

'Hello Mishu,' his mother was crying over phone.

'What happened, Mummy? Why are you crying like this?'

'Without delay, you come back. Daddy is in trouble and he needs your help.'

'Don't cry, I'm starting right now.' Medhansh put the phone down. Sara was standing behind him, awaiting his response.

'Sara, lock the house from inside. I'm leaving.'

'What about me? You know I can't stay alone.'

'Don't behave like a desi Indian woman, always dependent on a man. Grow up. You can be here or go to your parent's place.'

Medhansh quickly gathered some things in an overnight bag and headed out the front door. 'Bye, Sara, take care. I'll call you tomorrow.'

Sara took her car and rushed to her parents place that night. Her parents were worried to see her arrive there at that time of the night. When she narrated the whole incident they comforted her, and the focus shifted to the well-being of Medhansh's family.

It was nothing but the monetary help his family required to compensate for the losses. He could have waited till morning but it was just the hype created by his mother to show urgency. It was de-stressing for Medhansh to hear that the problem was only financial, and he promised them another ten lakh personal loan within seven days. He didn't even think once to call Sara and discuss the matter with her.

Medhansh was not wrong for his part. His love for his parents made him do whatever he could to satisfy them. As a son, he was justifying his part but as a husband he was unable to manage his role. He came back the next day and he and Sara fought over the issue. He expressed his helplessness and she cried about their future and one more day passed away.

The next day she became busy with her job and Medhansh also got involved in his work. But with each passing day there was a gap which was widening and Medhansh seemed unconcerned about it.

One evening, when Sara was rushing out of her office, she saw a guy standing in front of her office gate talking to someone but keeping an eye on every person moving out of the office. As she passed by him, she didn't pay heed to look at his face as she was in a hurry, but all of a sudden, maybe be it was her intuition, she raised her eyes to look at the person. He turned his face towards her and for a moment she was flabbergasted.

'Hi,' the guy said.

'Hi, Sidhant. How come you are here?'

'I work in the European bank head office near to your building.'

'When did you come back from the U.S.?'

Sidhant was just looking into Sara's eyes. 'It's been six months,' he said.

'What brought you here?'

Sidhant smiled, 'There are so many beautiful people here. Let's sit somewhere. Care for a cup of coffee?'

'Some other day. I have to rush back home,' Sara said with a perplexed mind.

'You are staying in the same Greater Kailash house?' he asked.

'No, I'm in Saket. Let's catch up some other time.'

'Ok, bye.' She rushed towards the parking lot.

Sara couldn't believe herself. As soon as she reached home the first thing she did was to share the story with Medhansh. Medhansh didn't say anything much, except, 'This is a small world.' However, his insecurities were back and he knew Sara was an emotional girl and she would require some attention now. For her part, Sara was relaxed in her mind and not finding herself on tenterhooks at seeing him. She was happy; she had gone beyond her feelings for Sidhant.

The next day, when she was entering her office complex, she again felt edgy. She started thinking about Sidhant and his eyes were haunting her. "Will he come to meet me anytime? Is he aware of my marriage?" and many more thoughts of the same nature. She reached her bay and after placing her laptop on the table, she stood near the window watching outside. She found herself all the more confused. There were several questions striking her mind like, "Why has he come back to India after studying at such a prestigious institute in the U.S.?"

The limited knowledge she had of him was that he wasn't too close to his family and they weren't bothered too much about him, so there wasn't any reason for him coming back due to family.

She started thinking that it must be due to the profile offered to him here. Moreover, it was an esteemed bank, so working there was a privilege.

Whatever it was, Sara was having sleepless nights thinking about it. She knew she was married and nothing was of relevance to her now, yet she was unable to control herself and was yielding under the stress. It became a daily ritual to pause in front of Sidhant's office, and then move forward to her own.

One day there was a call from reception at Sara's desk, 'Sara, Sidhant is here in the lobby to meet you.'

'I'm coming,' she replied.

Sara came to the reception area. The receptionist pointed towards Sidhant and Sara nodded. Sidhant had the same expressionless face. He was unable to take his eyes off of Sara.

'Naina, please issue him a visitor's pass; he's going inside with me.' She noted his identity and issued him a visitor's pass. Sara took him to her bay. There was silence for a moment.

'You look all the more depressed,' he said.

Sara wanted to tell him that he was the reason. 'No it's just; I'm a bit stressed out these days.'

'That day you said you have moved to Saket. Is everything okay with your parents?'

'Yes, they are fine. I have got married and I have moved with my husband,' Sidhant again showed no reaction. Sara felt as if he already knew it and he just wanted to hear it from her. It was challenging for Sara to tell him about her marriage. She felt as if she was losing him forever. She realized, of course, that they never had any relationship, but still she felt uncomfortable in facing this truth.

'Who's he?' he asked without emotion.

'He was my sister's senior.'

'Where did you meet him?'

'I met him due to my sister; at a friend's party. By the way, that friend of my sister is her hubby now.'

'When did it happen?'

'When I was in my final year,' Sara was answering his each and every question with precision. He, it seemed, was trying to analyze where did he drop the ball. It's unfortunate that to express our love we wait for the right opportunity and a right phase in our life-flow diagram. We tend to be God and try to interfere with this innocent, tender and natural feeling which can never be controlled. In this process at times, we mess up our whole lives. If Sidhant thought Sara would love her after MBA, then he was not looking for love but making himself more saleable. He had never expressed his love to her; maybe she would have died for that chameleon.

'What does he do for his living?'

'He's in IT.'

Sara took him to the cafeteria. Without asking him she ordered two black coffees.

'You still remember my taste.'

'I have a lot of memories of my classmates and our time there. I'll never forget it.'

Sidhant was quiet, as if all his interest in Sara had vanished. Sara kept talking for the heck of it. She knew the whole environment was embarrassing for her as well as for him. He finished his coffee, 'I'll leave. Sometime come to my office.'

'Sure.' He left the place leaving Sara confounded.

The next day, when Sara was going to her office her emotions were compelling her to make a visit to Sidhant's office rather than going to her own. She looked forward to meeting him. She experienced a kind of happiness with Sidhant which she had never felt with Medhansh. There's always a difference in heart beats when you are with a husband or when you are with a beau. She felt enchanted by Sidhant, a feeling which she had never been able to identify. However, she knew, she always liked to be with him; although, he had always been running away from her, or if not running away, certainly not doing anything to engender her closeness. Sara restrained herself for a couple of days, and then one day in the afternoon she barged into Sidhant's office. The receptionist informed her that he was out of town, and she came back to her own office disappointed. While she was coming out of his office, Abhimanyu saw her. Somehow, he gave her fishy looks and that made Sara uncomfortable. Usually, she used to tell everything to Medhansh but that evening she made a conscious effort to avoid telling him anything.

Sara knew that it was her turn now and she would have to make efforts if she wanted to talk to him. Next day she called up at his office and a lady replied, 'Ma'am, he's out of station.'

Sara called him again and this time he got on the line.

'Guess, who's calling?'

Sidhant was playing dumb. He could have recognized Sara's voice from any part of the world, but his ego made him pretend, 'Is that Raima?'

'Sorry, it's Sara.'

'Oh! Hi.'

'Sidhant, why don't you come to my office some day? I came to meet you but you weren't there and I don't feel comfortable coming again and again to your office.'

'Ok, I'll come next week.'

Sara wasn't sure if he would come. Anyways, it was relieving for Sara to find Sidhant happy and she felt absolved from her guilt of hurting Sidhant by being rude to him. Sara never gave a second thought when she said, 'No', to Rohit, Jimmy, Prateek and Abhimanyu. Their feelings never concerned her; however, when it came to Sidhant, she was very sensitive about him. She should have earlier questioned herself on her baggage of guilt. Was it pride or something else that never allowed Sara to question her true feelings about him? It was too late in the game and she was aware of the fact.

She used to discuss her feelings with Medhansh every day, which made him all the more insecure. Since the beginning, he had no doubts that she and Sidhant loved each other. It was their larger than life egos and even fear of failure, which kept them apart. Medhansh highly underestimated the intensity of their feelings, and his attitude of considering life a moving train had put all of them in trouble. Sidhant's coming back into their lives baffled Medhansh. At that time, Medhansh realized how much he loved Sara and the thought of losing her was making him crazy. He started becoming too caring and loving for Sara. Sara was finding his behavior too childish as she could understand what was going on in his mind.

At this time, Sara didn't really want to hear anything from Sidhant, and it wasn't because she was married or she had given a commitment to Medhansh but was due to Sidhant himself. She had always had a respect for him as a person; now by making him a second fiddle she didn't want to demean him in any way. She was also afraid, he might misunderstand that her feelings for him were due to the career progression he had made or the corroboration of his determination and stability he had produced.

Medhansh had to take another personal loan to pay for his father's losses. He went back to his home, gave his father the money and settled all the issues related to the rejected consignment. His father was not keeping well since the time he heard about his business loss. Medhansh was worried about it. His elder brother was bothered more about his wife's reaction to their deteriorated financial condition and he was of no support to the parents, so in the end Medhansh was the one who had to take all the onus of their emotional and financial distress. He tried to do whatever he could by giving assurances of all sorts.

Sara was finding Medhansh to be physically present with her but emotionally and mentally he was always preoccupied. He would "hear" and not listen to her. Sara had started feeling a void in her life. She had never felt felicity in her marriage. She thought time would bring them closer, and one day she would realize that he was her love.

As promised, Sidhant came to meet Sara in her office. It was lunch time.

'Hi, how are you?' Sidhant asked Sara with an obsessive look.

'I'm good, feeling better after seeing you.' Sara was losing control over herself or she wanted to be honest. Sidhant blushed; he didn't know how to be flirtatious with girls as he was a matter of fact kind.

'Did you have lunch?'

'No, I'll have it after going from here.'

'Let's go out somewhere.'

'You want to go with me?'

Sara could feel the ache in Sidhant's heart which gave her a sickening feeling. The maturity Sidhant had gained over the years helped him to sound curious but not sarcastic. 'Of course with you. Don't worry we'll be going dutch.' she said. 'I heard you never sponsored anyone in the college.'

'Yes,' he replied. 'Because I was always short of funds,' he was extremely graceful. Sidhant was a simple guy with little flamboyance. He was interested in good food and not in the place where he was having it. Sara took him to a nearby small restaurant; a neat and tidy place, where there was little chance of being disturbed by someone. They ordered simple, north Indian food.

Sidhant was silent for most of the time. This compelled Sara to say something; otherwise they would just sit quiet, so at times she was being quirky. Sidhant was simply looking in her eyes. Sara wasn't able to understand what he was trying to find out. She tried diverting his attention.

'How was your stay at school?'

'It's a fantastic institution; you get an entire new perspective of looking at things.'

'How did you find REC?'

'It was good, it could have been better,' he smiled, but Sara couldn't make out what he was trying to tell, and neither did she ask him to elaborate.

'Sara, I'm moving back to the U.S.'

'The U.S.??? Why did you come back at the first place?' Sara was sounding angry as if he was going to do some blunder.

'You are right, I shouldn't have come back. But you know, I'm an emotional person who doesn't accept changes so easily. I spent two years there; it was an uphill task, as I always missed my friends and this environment.'

'What happened now?' Sara asked coming out of the shock.

'I'm finding a very unprofessional and laid back environment here. Now, I'm realizing after getting accustomed to the work ethics of the U.S., it's difficult to work here.'

'Won't it be too far away from your parents?' Sara actually wanted to say, from her.

'No, I feel emotionally if you are attached to each other, distances are immaterial.' When anybody talked to him about his parents, he was unable to hide his distance from them. Sara all of a sudden, started feeling sulky.

'Are you in touch with anyone in our batch?' Sidhant asked

'You mean to ask about Jimmy. You thought I was quite pally with him'. The thought of Sidhant moving away from her made her uncomfortable so she started reacting in an erratic manner.

'No, I didn't mean it. I feel we have grown over the years.'

'Last time, I met everyone was at Avni and Jimmy's marriage.' There wasn't any reaction from Sidhant.

'You know,' she continued. 'Avni and Jimmy finally got married.'

'Ya, Jimmy called me up.' said Sidhant.

Sara could make out from his face that he was keeping his fingers on the pulse of their batch. He should have been aware of her as well. Sara was wondering, "Why is he sitting in front of me now. How could he have allowed me to marry someone else if he loved me? How can he muddle the whole life?"

Sidhant wouldn't say so, of course, but he was in constant touch with Jimmy to keep track of Sara. He assumed that as Avni and Sara were good friends, Sara would be sharing everything with Avni, and Jimmy would further pass on the information to him.

He couldn't have even imagined in his faintest dream that Avni and Jimmy had decided not to share this news with him, though he knew they never had a good opinion about him. It was only a month back when he met Rohit that he came to know about Sara's marriage.

They finished their lunch. 'Let's go back to my office,' Sara said. She wanted Sidhant to be with her for some more time.

'No, I would go now. I need to hand over a few things before I leave.'

'When are you flying?' Sara waited for his answer with a thumping heart.

'This weekend.'

Sidhant accompanied Sara back to her office. They didn't realize it but there was a pin drop silence between them as the two of them waited for each other to say something.

'Okay, it's time to say good-bye,' Sidhant told Sara with stoned eyes. He wanted to hold her in his arms and never let her go anywhere but pride follows its own way....

'Would we be in touch after this?' Sara got emotional and couldn't hide her emotions. Her eyes were red and voice became heavy. Her face simply said one thing, 'please don't go away!'

Sidhant could read her, 'Wherever I am, I'll always know about you.' He knew she was having a conflict within herself and she would be addled as usual.

'Bye,' said Sara and she started walking inside the office.

Sidhant consoled himself on his decision of returning back to the U.S. That day he was sure that Sara loved him more than ever. He also knew that she would not leave her marriage nor would she now accept her love for him. *It was his love for her which prompted him to move away from her, so that she's peaceful and undivided; although, he knew she could never be happy.*

It was also impossible for him to exist, with Sara being perceived to be around him, but not with him. He knew there was nothing much left in his life. MBA was just a means to get closer to her and was never his aim.

⁂

When she reached home, Medhansh found her melancholy, 'You are looking too beautiful today. Did Sidhant come to meet you?'

'Rubbish, what the hell do my looks have to do with Sidhant? Anyways, he did come,' Medhansh knew she was again running away from reality, but now it was in the best interest of everyone.

Medhansh was smart enough to handle her, and this was one thing Sara liked about him. He prepared dinner for her and took her out for a long drive. Sara felt relatively better. Within him, Medhansh was breathing a sigh of relief. He considered Sidhant gone forever.

Medhansh got a call from home that day about his father's ill health. He had to immediately leave for his home. He asked Sara to stay back as he knew she had few meetings lined up for the next day.

Medhansh called up Sara in the morning, 'Papa is too stressed out. His blood pressure isn't getting under control. He's under medical observation right now. I'm trying to do my best.'

Sara panicked, 'Should I send Mamma there?'

'No need, our family doctor is taking care of him. In case it's required, I'll let you know.'

'Okay, bye, take care.'

Medhansh's father continued to show no sign of improvement for the next two days. She was in constant touch with Medhansh and provided full moral support to him.

It was Friday and Sara was exceptionally busy at the office. At around 2 p.m., she received a call from Sidhant. 'Hi, I thought I'll talk to you before leaving.'

'Nice of you.'

'You seem to be quite busy nowadays; going back home quite late.'

Sara didn't understand the purpose of this interest now and anyways, she was too disturbed, 'Ya, it's too hectic these days. Moreover, Medhansh isn't here so I get additional time to spend in the office.'

'Are you getting along well with your husband?'

Sara found it too absurd. She couldn't understand what prompted him to say that, 'I have married a man of my choice so in any case I have to be always with him.'

Sidhant understood, she wasn't prepared to accept her emotions. She was too committed, but hoping against hopes, he couldn't stop himself from taking a last chance.

He was skeptical about the intensity of her relationship with her husband as he also believed that she couldn't have loved anyone. His perception about her was the reason he took his sweet time to approach her. He had always liked her for her dedication in whatever she did. It always made him believe that if she loved someone it could be a feeling no one would have ever experienced before. However, whether she could love someone always left a big question mark in his mind but now he was sure she loved him.

'I wish you all the best!' said Sidhant finally.

'Take care, bye,' Sara was relieved that at last, she had made her mind clear to him. She assumed, she had closed this chapter of their lives.

CHAPTER 13

SARA RECEIVED A CALL from Medhansh, 'Sara, Papa is very critical. Please come here immediately.'

'I'm coming.' She rushed to Medhansh's parent's house. Before she could reach there, his father passed away due to massive heart attack. On his side, Medhansh was grieved by his father's sudden demise, at that young age and on the other end, the whole family came into a topsy-turvy state. Medhansh was now the sole bread earner of the family.

Sara was there for a few days with Medhansh, until all the rites were performed. Medhansh was emotionally wrecked. She decided to give maximum support to him. Medhansh was busy settling his family affairs and Sara had to get back to work as she could not justify too long an absence from the office.

There was hardly any honeymoon period for Medhansh and Sara. Destiny had been challenging them from the very first day. Sara started focusing more and more on her career as there wasn't anything else to do, and Medhansh started spending maximum time with his family and job due to his ultimate love for them. After his father passed, he got all the more attached to his mother. If there was anything which disturbed her, it perturbed Medhansh beyond limits.

The latest issue of constant bickering at his parental home was between his mother and his elder brother's wife, Supriya. Sometimes she wanted to throw a party and another time she demanded a holiday abroad. His brother could have never afforded to annoy his wife. Mohit was now and then pestering his mother for financial help from Medhansh.

Medhansh obliged by sending money for his brother's extravagances to keep his mother pacified. Time was taking its course, and on one pretext or the other Sara and Medhansh were moving away from each other. Sara wanted to talk to Medhansh about their relationship whenever they could afford some time together; however, their relationship had taken a back seat for Medhansh, and he was more interested in discussing loan repayments and EMI's with her. This further strained their relationship and constant fights became norm of their life.

Sara was under the continuous stress of a decaying relationship. She found him an opportunist. *She wasn't bogged down by the hardships she had to face with Medhansh but due to his completely new facet of love. Sara wasn't able to answer herself, if Medhansh ever loved her as he claimed, or was she the best available option to him at the time.*

Her parents were a constant morale support to Sara. They realized very early in their daughter's marriage that it was a mistake; the two young people had different values and levels of commitment. But then, it was their daughter's decision and they respected it.

Sara was doing very well in her career. She was progressing by leaps and bounds. An opportunity in the U.S. came her way where she had to work as an executive assistant to Abhimanyu. Sara didn't show any inclination to accept this opportunity; neither was there was any compulsion to take it. It wasn't because of Abhimanyu; he was quite a professional man. She was disinterested as she knew going away from Medhansh would further widen the gap between them. Still, she discussed it with Medhansh.

Medhansh was so excited to hear it, 'Sara, you must go! It can be a milestone in your career and who knows, after some time you can also call me there.' Medhansh was trying hard for an overseas opportunity but wasn't successful.

So Sara decided to go for it. Diya and Ankit were also there, so she thought she would get a chance to meet them too.

Abhimanyu was a reserved personality, only preferring to talk business. Sara knew this very well, and had no issues with this, as she also wanted to be quiet because of her mental state.

The position was in Simi Valley, California. It was a beautiful place and the weather was awesome. Sara took an apartment at a little distance from Abhimanyu. Sara and Abhimanyu were phlegmatic to each other. She settled down well with her new job profile.

Abhimanyu was a vegetarian and it was becoming difficult for him to survive there on hash potatoes and bread. He was craving for home food. With no choice left, he asked Sara, 'Are you okay here, any problems?'

'I'm fine, thanks.'

'How do you manage food?' he asked.

It was shocking for Sara to find Abhimanyu getting concerned about her food. 'I cook it at my apartment. Although, I'm a non-vegetarian, but still I find it difficult to sustain on outside stuff.'

'Wonderful! But I'm a vegetarian. I was thinking if I can assist you in preparing vegetarian food and then we can share it. I'm not a fussy eater; I can eat whatever you prepare.'

'I cook only in the evenings.'

'Good! Straight from the office I can accompany you to your apartment.'

'Okay.'

Sara wasn't missing Medhansh at this time and she usually avoided calling him. Whenever she called or Medhansh rang up, it was a casual talk with complete disinterest from Sara, and Medhansh being more interested in talking about their U.S. plans.

Abhimanyu was acting as a good assistant to Sara. Very soon he realized, she wasn't an expert cook like his mother, but she just managed it nicely. He was happy that he was getting some variety to eat. While in the kitchen they hardly spoke to each other. They didn't intrude in each other's personal space, so they preferred to have dinner separately at their apartments. After food was ready, he used to pack and leave.

One evening as they were in the kitchen preparing food Abhimanyu asked Sara, 'Are you upset?'

'No, why do you say so?'

'I can see it on your face. When I met you for the first time during training, at that time also I didn't find you very happy, but now you look despondent.'

'Abhimanyu, there's nothing like it. Anyways, thanks for your concern.'

He wanted to lighten the stress which was created in the environment, 'Maybe you are missing your hubby.'

Sara smiled; Abhimanyu was smart enough to see a pain in her smile.

Sara took a day off on Friday, and flew to New Jersey to meet Diya and Ankit. She tried her best to create three days inventory for Abhimanyu while she was gone. He was touched by her efforts. He had all the more started liking her for her simplicity and sincerity. Abhimanyu was happy that she was taking a weekend to see her sister and dropped her off at the airport.

When she reached JFK airport, Diya and Ankit were there to receive her. Sara's emotions overpowered her and she started crying at seeing them. She hugged them so tightly and her tears were not stopping for any reason. The two of them could feel that she wasn't the same Sara; she seemed a shattered person. Ankit could guess the reason. He preferred not to broach any discussion about her personal life unless she brought it up. He knew Sara wasn't the kind of person who would discuss her personal life with anyone.

Anyway, her weekend with her relatives in New Jersey was pleasant. It was a good change and she felt calmer after it.

When she got back to California, Abhimanyu told her, 'Sara, there's a very good opportunity. A banker's meet has been organized here in Simi Valley to present their white papers on "Use of technology in the banking system." I'm sure you can write something innovative on the kind of work you have been doing and I can forward your name for the presentation.'

Abhimanyu was excited about it, and he encouraged Sara. She agreed to participate. Sara prepared a draft and after rounds of reviews by the committee appointed by bank, the paper got approval after a month of hard work. It was a five day conference and representatives from the world over were coming to participate.

On day one of the conference, Abhimanyu and Sara went to the opening presentations of the conference. The second day was Sara's scheduled day to present her paper. She was ready and when she raised herself to move towards the stage after her name was announced, Abhimanyu held her hand, 'Best of luck! I'm sure, it's going to be the best.'

'Thanks,' and she marched towards the stage.

She started her presentation and suddenly got an eyeful of Sidhant sitting in the extreme right corner of that big conference hall. She couldn't have been more surprised! He was looking at Sara with his usual vacuous face and eyes stuck on her. Sara became overly self-conscious and started losing track during her presentation. It disturbed Abhimanyu to the extent that he got up from his place and started moving out of the room to find Sidhant there. Sidhant and Abhimanyu were alumni of the same school; Abhimanyu knew him through the alumni network. Abhimanyu receded and went back to his chair. He could see now Sara fixated with the man, while trying not to appear so. Sidhant was sitting there as if inebriated. All this was sufficient for Abhimanyu to draw some conclusions.

Sara finished her presentation and a round of applause followed her. When she came back to her place, Abhimanyu simply nodded at her without saying anything. She knew, she had goofed up and was already feeling embarrassed.

Abhimanyu murmured, 'Is he your husband?'

Sara knew whom he was talking about, 'No.'

They were quiet after that. During lunch hour, Sara and Sidhant exchanged smiles. Sidhant said, 'Hi,' to Abhimanyu and he also got involved in a small chat with him. Sara was wondering about their connection. She asked Sidhant to join them for lunch. No one spoke to each other during lunch. Abhimanyu could see Sidhant finding it very difficult to take his eyes off Sara.

When they were going back to the conference room, Abhimanyu asked,

'Sara, Is he the cause of your stress?'

'Who? Sidhant?'

'You know what I'm saying.'

'No, he was just my classmate in engineering.'

'I can see that from your faces.'

'By the way, how do you know him?' she asked.

'I'm an alumnus of his school.'

'Oh!'

'Do you mind taking dinner with me today?'

'Sure, I hope we aren't going to discuss Sidhant.'

'Hmmm.....'

They went out to an Indian Restaurant, 'Little India'. It wasn't food on his mind but something else. He genuinely wanted to help Sara as he could feel she required it urgently. As soon as they were seated there, 'Why didn't you marry him?'

'Excuse me?'

'I'm saying, why you didn't marry Sidhant. From what I can guess, it shouldn't be any family issue.'

'There were so many boys in my class; you mean to say I should have married every one.'

'Stop bullshitting,' Abhimanyu got furious as if some subordinate was trying to play him for a fool. Boss is boss after all!

'There wasn't anything between us.' she said.

'You should have seen your eyes in front of him, and he too. You guys are mad about each other.'

'He never said anything like it.'

'What about you?' he said. 'You are an Indian girl, so how could you have? I thought you to be an intelligent and mature girl. You know when you said, "No", to me, I really felt like losing something precious. I considered you'll be an asset in anyone's life. I'm astonished to find out you are a foolish, egotistic brat.'

'Oh! That's a long list of adjectives,' Sara remarked without further reacting to Abhimanyu.

'Sara, don't be jocular. Grow up! High time you should streamline your life.'

Sara commented, 'What can I do? Man, whom I married, and who claimed to have loved me, doesn't have even an idea of what love is and on the other side, the man whom you say I'm madly in love with, has been always moving in circles and has never expressed himself. I don't have any idea about his last three years.'

'Talk to him....'

'It's not possible. I'm married and have many commitments. Moreover, if he had something in his heart, he should have told me.'

'Sara, you are sailing in many boats. If you are so committed then he shouldn't be even there in your thoughts.'

'He isn't. I don't know how come he's here, is it by chance or intentional? I have always been bewildered about his intentions.'

'Please, don't tell me he isn't there with you. You almost created a scene during the presentation; and look at him, he is no different.'

Sara blushed.

'Look at you, your face is turning red! And you tell me, you aren't concerned. At least be honest to yourself. I'm sorry, I have intruded in your personal life because I like you and want good for you. Sara, you are trapped in a vicious circle. I don't know whether you love your husband or not, but you don't want to hurt him. You are afraid to hurt your ego by knowing Sidhant's true feelings and he's afraid to expose him. Please help yourself, come out of this chaos. It can cost you your life.'

The dinner was too taxing for Sara. She knew Abhimanyu was right in his thoughts. She wished that he could have suggested to her the way out.

Sara and Sidhant met a few times at the conference. They hardly spoke to each other. She was with Abhimanyu most of the time.

Sidhant hadn't changed a bit. It was impossible for him not to look at Sara. Several times Sara and Abhimanyu observed him staring at her; they exchanged glances and then Abhimanyu tried to ignore it, to avoid further embarrassment to her.

Abhimanyu and Sara completed their assignment in the U.S. and it was time to go back home.

Medhansh was there to receive Sara, at the Indira Gandhi International airport, New Delhi. He was eager to meet Sara after such a long time. Sara was hopeful that this separation would add a new life to their relationship except this shocking appearance of Sidhant in the U.S. had thrown her into a spin.

'Oh my loving wife, you don't know how much I missed you.' Sara wanted to believe that he really missed her, and he was not just being cheesy.

He was also curious to discuss her long term prospects in the U.S.

'Medhansh, maybe we can discuss it some other time.'

'Sure sweetheart. How are Ankit and Diya?'

'They are planning to come back.'

'Why? Are they fools?'

'What's wrong in it?' she said. 'They are missing family there.'

'Okay, it's their wish.'

'How's your family?'

'I forgot to tell you one thing; mummy and Supriya are having a tough time staying together, so I have planned to buy a new house for mummy near our ancestral home.'

'You forgot to tell me, or you avoided.'

'Please don't start it again. They are my family and I have to take care of them.'

'Does it mean, they'll have the entire extravaganza in life and they won't do any adjustments either, and would you keep financing them? You already have tremendous debt on you, how can you plan to buy a new house?'

'My dear wife, it would be your house. It would be in your name and Mummy would just stay there.'

'But who is going to arrange the finances?' Sara knew he was going to say something which she could have never ever expected him to think.

'You'll take the home loan, and I'll help you in repaying it.'

This was exactly what she felt he was about to say. Sara was under a state of shock. She had never imagined him to be such a self-centered and manipulative person. She kept quiet because she had no words for Medhansh's shamelessness, and he considered silence as half consent. He thought he was well equipped with all the techniques of making it a full consent.

'Sara, I need to rush in the morning to meet some brokers. They have identified some properties.'

As soon as they reached home, Medhansh used his magical charm to woo her. He carried her to the bedroom, as soon as he put her on the bed and was coming closer to her, she pushed him back.

'What has happened Sara? We are meeting after such a long time.'

'I have a headache and I'm too tired. I want to sleep.' She switched off the light and turned her face to the other side of the bed, pretending as if she was sleeping. Medhansh felt too humiliated as he knew she was avoiding him.

Without saying anything to her, he left in the morning. Sara didn't sleep the whole night and she was waiting for him to go out.

The next day, after office, Sara went to her parent's place. Sara's mother could see the increased tension on her face but there was no point discussing it with her every time, as it made her more restless. She wanted her to have peaceful time there. They discussed Ankit and Diya. Both Mamma and Papa were amused to hear about their life. Their plan of returning back to India thrilled them. Sara felt more relaxed.

It was a happy night for her.

'Sara, crush some six cloves of garlic. Be quick! After that finely chop these mushrooms and capsicums.'

'And what are you going to do?'

'I'm the chef. I'll prepare white pasta for you.'

'Sidhant, you haven't changed. You are as lethargic as you always were.'

'Better focus on what I have told you to do; otherwise, do it yourself.'

'Ok, don't act so pricey,'

Sara woke up to realize that it was a dream where she was with Sidhant in the U.S., and he was there preparing the white pasta and she was assisting him. Whatever it was, she woke up with a smile on her face. Mamma was satisfied to find her smiling.

Sara went back to her home at Saket in the evening. Medhansh was not at home yet. He came late at night and she had fallen asleep by that time.

A few days passed by and it was back to the monotonous routine. Sara and Medhansh avoided getting face to face. Then one evening, Medhansh came in a little early as Sara was preparing dinner.

'Hi Sara. Are you annoyed with me?' Before she could say anything, 'Can we have dinner together?'

'I'm laying down the table, you get freshened up.'

Medhansh was back within five minutes. Sara was at the dining table waiting for him.

'You wanted to talk to me.'

'I didn't say that. It's been days since we had dinner together,' Medhansh said in his usual cheesy tone.

'You haven't said anything and I'm sure you want to talk to me about something,' Sara was sarcastic.

Medhansh smiled, 'You know me so well. I have applied for a home loan from ICICI Bank. There are a few documents which I require from you and you also need to sign at some places.'

'Excuse me,' Sara got up from the dining table exasperated, and straight away went to their bed room and bolted it from the inside.

Medhansh knocked on the door several times, but Sara didn't respond, so he slept in the living room.

Sara was weeping the whole night. A strong girl like her should have rebuffed him a long time ago. Somehow, depression was gripping her and she didn't realize it. She became submissive and every small thing shattered her. It was a mixed bag of feelings. She was perplexed due to Sidhant as well.

Sara didn't realize when she fell asleep.

Beep, beep....

The phone woke her up. 'Hello Sara, Sidhant here.'

'Hi.'

'Are you okay? Last night I saw you in my dream and you were crying. This has happened to me for the first time. I hope you are fine.'

'Sidhant, this is too childish. You should have thought of a different excuse to call me.' Sara hung up the phone.

Sara heard Medhansh locking the main door. She came out of the room to find loan papers lying on the dining table with a note written, 'I hope you'll grow up and regain your sanity. Please sign at the places marked with a cross.'

It was a moment and Sara got too frustrated. On one end, she had developed an aversion for Medhansh and on the other hand, Sidhant's attitude was killing her. She took a paper and started scribbling on it:

You can live with a mistake
But what, if you have made a blunder,
Every moment, it makes me realize how wrong I was?
I need to give it a pause,
I'm a weak person; who can't take it anymore,
Whatever I had, has been torn,
I want to be freed,
Hey you man! Open your doors,

After a life I'm coming to meet you, to soothe your sores
To tell you, 'I love you.'

She placed the paper on the side table and gulped an entire bottle of sleeping pills.

In a few moments, the main door opened. It was Medhansh. He had left his cell phone in the living room, plugged in for charging. While he was picking up the phone, there was bell at the door. It was Sara's mother. She was coming back from some emergency call and on the way thought of meeting her daughter.

Medhansh opened the door.

'Hello, Mamma.'

'How are you, Medhansh? Going to office, so early in the morning.'

'No, I'm going to meet some property dealers.'

'Sara didn't tell me. You guys are planning to buy a house?'

Medhansh was glad to know that Sara was not sharing everything with her mother. Veering from the topic, Medhansh asked, 'Mamma, would you like to have tea?'

'If I'm not bothering you, yes. Where's Sara?'

'She's sleeping. Please go inside; meanwhile, I'll prepare tea for you and Sara.' Medhansh had this acumen of turning cheesy whenever required.

'Sara, Sara....' Mamma opened the bedroom door. She saw Sara lying on the bed. Being a doctor, she identified that Sara was unconscious. She rushed to her; checked her pulse and looked into her eyes. She was alive. Mamma breathed a sigh of relief! She immediately called up the ambulance. Medhansh came in running as soon as he heard her say ambulance. He was astonished to see Sara lying in that condition.

'What happened to her Mamma?'

'Please keep quiet. You have done your job, let me do mine. Do me a favor; bring a glass of water and salt, quickly!'

Medhansh rushed to the kitchen and got it with in a fraction of second. Mamma tried stomach lavaging using salt water but it was in vain. She looked around and saw a note lying on the side table. She picked it up and her eyes were in tears. Mamma kept it in her purse.

The ambulance arrived and Mamma rushed Sara to her clinic. There was a doctor in the ambulance who got a charcoal neutralizer as instructed by Mamma. The doctor gave it to her on the way to neutralize the effect of the drug. As soon as they reached the clinic, intravenous fluid was started to wash the bloodstream. After a while, Mamma realized that her daughter was responding to the treatment. Her pulse was returning to normal.

Mamma moved out of the room and checked Sara's mobile log. The last dialed call was to her office at around 8:30 p.m. the previous night. One call was received in the morning from an international number. She called back on the number.

'Sidhant,' Mamma immediately got some clarity on the matter.

'Hi, this is Sara's mother.'

Before she could say anything, Sidhant asked, 'What happened to her? Is she okay?'

'No, she's fighting for her life.' Mamma told him about Sara's act.

'I was so restless since morning. I had a premonition that something wrong was going to happen to her. There was something nagging her mind and making her depressed, and I called her in the morning to ask her about her welfare. I feel that's what made her maudlin and in impulse, she tried getting rid of all her sorrows.'

'I don't know what relationship you have with Sara or maybe I'm getting too hasty. If you have something in mind, come immediately to my place otherwise close this chapter forever,' Mamma hung up the phone.

After five hours or so, Mamma declared Sara to be out of danger. Medhansh and her father were present in the room. Her father couldn't control himself and burst into tears, 'How could she think of such a nasty act? Nothing is bigger than life. She even didn't think about us, and took a decision in a moment. It's not only her life! We have sacrificed our lives to raise her and today we are living, to see our kids live happily. If something was troubling her mind she could have discussed with us. She has shattered our faith; I have failed to raise my kids properly.' He was unable to control his tears.

Mamma gave him a light hug, 'Think about me, she has massacred my feelings too. We'll have to be patient at the time.'

When things were a bit pacified, Medhansh said to Mamma, 'I have a few urgent things to be completed today. If both of you are here, can I go to the office? I'll come as soon as possible.'

Mamma instantly remarked, 'Please go and finish your work. There's no haste; anyways, I would not like anyone to disturb her for another twelve hours.' As an obedient boy, Medhansh took the instructions and moved out of the room.

'Mamma, Mamma,' Sara murmured and then again she closed her eyes. Mamma rushed towards her. She was looking so frail. Her white color got a yellowish tinge. There was peace on her face. Mamma burst into tears. Her angel wanted to die to get this peace.

She was waiting anxiously for Sidhant to arrive.

Sara gained her consciousness. Mamma and Papa kissed her on her cheeks, forehead and hugged her. Her eyes were restless. Mamma knew she wanted to avoid Medhansh and she was ensuring that he wasn't around.

'My sweetheart, don't worry about anything. Just try to feel happy. This is a new life for you and it'll have everything you want. I'm sure, if I and your papa can't bring a smile to your face, is there someone who can?'

'Who?' Sara said softly.

'Should I call Abhimanyu?'

'No! No! Don't even tell him,' Sara said in a broken voice.

'Don't worry, I'm not going to do anything; you just relax.' Mamma waited for her to ask for Medhansh, but she didn't show any interest in him.

Medhansh came back in the evening and he had also called Mamma in between to ask about her welfare. Mamma took the same stand; she was sleeping and should be left alone.

Sara was in a subconscious state for almost twelve hours. Her mother preferred her to sleep and take complete rest. Actually she wanted to give some time to Sidhant.

The next day, at 10 p.m., a tall wheat-ish guy appeared at Mamma's clinic carrying a big bag, he was looking a little disheveled. He asked about Sara's mother. Medhansh could recognize him in less than a second as he had seen him in Sara's class group photograph. His presence baffled him. Before Medhansh could talk to him, Mamma came out, 'I'm Sara's mother.'

Sidhant folded his hands and nodded at her. She knew he was Sidhant. She took him to an adjacent room, 'Are you married, Sidhant?'

'No, how can I? I promised your daughter that I'll wait for her.'

After listening to him, she handed over the Sara's suicide note to him. As soon as he read it, it seemed, as if fresh blood had started flowing into his veins. He knew she had written about him, and Mamma could feel that she hadn't made a mistake by calling him there.

'Sidhant, I'm not sure whether this is love for you or abhorrence for her husband.'

'I know, this is only and only love for me. I could have waited lifelong to hear it from her, and that it would come in this way was beyond my imagination.'

'I don't understand why you guys never expressed your feelings to each other. Let me tell you one thing very clearly, you can meet her, only if you are ready to forgo your ego and accept her as she is. She's already gone through a lot of pain.'

'I promise you, I'll handle it this time.' Sidhant took out a, fresh from the garden, rose bouquet from his bag with deliriously rich fragrance.

There was a big smile on Mamma's face and she took him to Sara's room. Sara was lying there with her eyes closed. Sidhant paused at the door and started looking at her, one thing he couldn't have stopped himself from was staring at her and he was also mustering the courage to go inside.

Mamma said, 'You can go inside and look at her.'

What Mamma said was shocking for Medhansh, and he came rushing towards the door but Mamma kept a hand in front of the door, blocking his way inside.

'Mamma, I'm her husband.'

'Medhansh, please let her live....'

New facet of love begins...............